THE BROKEN BRIDGE

Dr. Francis S. Laari

Kravitz & Sons

INNOVATORS IN PUBLISHING, MARKETING AND ADVERTISING

Kravitz and Sons LLC
204 E Arlington Blvd. Suite B
Greenville, NC 27858

Published by Kravitz and Sons LLC.
ISBN: 979-8-89639-713-7 (sc)
ISBN: 979-8-89639-712-0 (e)

TABLE OF CONTENTS

CHAPTER I

Introduction: The Broken Bridge Metaphor

The Middle East is a land of contrasts. It is a cradle of civilization, a mosaic of cultures, religions, and languages that stretch back millennia. It is a region that has given the world remarkable achievements in philosophy, science, art, and governance. Yet, it is also a landscape marked by the enduring scars of conflict, displacement, and human suffering. Cities that once bustled with commerce and culture—Aleppo, Baghdad, Sana'a, Gaza—now stand as testaments to the destructive consequences of war. Families are divided, neighborhoods erased, and generations are burdened with traumas inherited from conflicts they did not choose.

It is against this backdrop that *The Broken Bridge* seeks to explore both the history of destruction and the potential for reconstruction. This book is not simply a chronicle of violence or a catalog of geopolitical failures. It is an inquiry into the human, social, and moral dimensions of conflict—the ways war fractures communities, disrupts economies, and leaves moral and psychological ruptures that persist long after the last bomb falls. It examines how these fractures have created "broken bridges"—not just literal infrastructure destroyed by warfare, but also the social, cultural, and ethical connections between people that have been severed by decades of violence.

Yet, even as it confronts the darkness of destruction, this book is rooted in the possibility of hope and resilience. It demonstrates that amid the rubble, human ingenuity and courage endure. Women in refugee camps restore education and health services; youth reclaim abandoned lands, rebuild schools, and harness technology to document survival and foster dialogue; communities find ways to reconcile and rebuild trust even in areas long defined by division. These acts, often small and unnoticed on a global scale, constitute the essential threads of what this book calls "bridge-building"—the restoration of connections that war has severed.

The purpose of this book is therefore twofold. First, it seeks to illuminate the reality of conflict in the Middle East in its full complexity. Wars in Palestine, Syria, Yemen, Iraq, and beyond are not abstract events; they are lived experiences. They shape identities, influence political structures, and disrupt every facet of daily life. By highlighting stories of refugees, displaced families, children growing up amid rubble, and communities navigating scarcity and trauma, the book grounds geopolitical analysis in the human experience. It shows that the consequences of war extend far beyond statistics—they echo through generations, creating psychological, social, and moral fissures that demand attention.

Second, the book seeks to offer a vision for rebuilding and reconciliation. Conflict is not the only defining characteristic of the Middle East. The resilience of communities, the dedication of women and youth as agents of change, and the moral frameworks offered by local and international peacebuilding efforts reveal a path forward. Drawing lessons from global examples such as South Africa's Truth and Reconciliation Commission, Rwanda's gacaca courts, and Northern Ireland's local reconciliation initiatives, the book demonstrates that repair is possible, even in the most deeply scarred societies.

The narrative emphasizes that reconstruction is multidimensional. It is not merely about rebuilding roads, schools, or hospitals—it is about restoring human dignity, trust, and opportunity. It integrates economic recovery, climate-smart infrastructure, education, and technology, highlighting how each dimension contributes to the restoration of social and moral bridges. By showcasing local initiatives alongside broader systemic strategies, the book makes clear that peacebuilding is a collaborative endeavor. Ordinary people, local leaders, women, and youth are not peripheral actors—they are central to repairing the torn fabric of society.

Ultimately, the purpose of *The Broken Bridge* is to provide both understanding and action. It challenges readers to engage with the Middle East not only as a distant theater of conflict but as a living, breathing society where decisions, investments, and compassion can change the course of history. It invites reflection on moral responsibility, empathy, and the agency of local communities, and it encourages concrete steps—supporting local initiatives, investing in education, promoting dialogue, and advocating for holistic policies.

This book, therefore, is both a mirror and a map: a mirror reflecting the deep fractures caused by decades of conflict, and a map pointing toward the unbroken bridges that communities can rebuild. It asks its readers to witness the human consequences of war, understand the intricate web of social, political, and environmental challenges, and participate in the moral labor of reconstruction. Above all, it underscores a simple but profound truth: broken bridges can be repaired, and even in the midst of devastation, hope, agency, and resilience persist.

The history of the Middle East is a story of conflict—but the future need not be. By understanding the past, recognizing the human cost, and engaging in deliberate acts of bridge-building, societies can reconnect, heal, and flourish. This is the promise and the purpose of this book: to illuminate both the darkness of conflict and the possibility of a brighter, connected, and resilient Middle East.

The Symbol of a Bridge

Bridges are among the most enduring symbols of human civilization. They represent more than architecture; they represent the belief that separation is not destiny, that division can be overcome.

In Istanbul, the Bosporus Bridge stretches across continents, linking Europe and Asia. In San Francisco, the Golden Gate Bridge is not only an engineering marvel but also a cultural icon, symbolizing opportunity and openness. In New York, the Brooklyn Bridge was once called the "eighth wonder of the world," connecting communities and symbolizing the city's dynamism.

But bridges are not just monuments of progress. They also carry cultural and moral meaning. In Bosnia, the destruction of the Mostar Bridge during the Balkan wars became a global image of hatred. When it was rebuilt, it stood not only as stone across a river but as a testimony to the possibility of reconciliation.

The Middle East has long been a natural bridge—geographically, culturally, and spiritually. It is where Asia, Africa, and Europe meet. It is where Judaism, Christianity, and Islam began, each offering teachings of justice, mercy, and peace. It has been the corridor of empires, the stage of prophets, the marketplace of civilizations. Yet today, that bridge is broken.

Checkpoints, walls, and divisions have replaced the free flow of people and culture. Suspicion and hostility dominate where trust once existed. The "broken bridge" is not an abstract metaphor—it is the lived experience of millions.

Broken Promises, Broken Lives

The broken bridge is not just about physical barriers; it is also about the failure of promises.

After World War I, colonial powers promised independence but instead carved the region into artificial states through the Sykes-Picot Agreement. In the aftermath of World War II, Jewish refugees fleeing the Holocaust were promised a homeland, but Palestinians were simultaneously promised their right to land and sovereignty. The result was a tragedy of competing promises that set the stage for decades of war.

The Oslo Accords of 1993 raised hopes for peace between Israelis and Palestinians. Leaders shook hands on the White House lawn, and for a moment, the bridge seemed possible. But the process collapsed under mistrust, violence, and political failure. For Palestinians, Oslo became another broken promise; for Israelis, another bitter disappointment.

The Arab Spring of 2011 was yet another promise of dignity and reform. In Tunisia, progress was made. But in Syria, Libya, and Yemen, uprisings descended into chaos, leaving societies in rubble. Once again, the bridge of trust between people and leaders was shattered.

Each broken promise deepens cynicism. Families displaced in 1948 still live in camps labeled "temporary." Refugees from Iraq and Syria raise children who have never seen their ancestral homes. A Palestinian child in Gaza grows up not expecting peace but preparing for the next war. A Yemeni mother watches her children starve not because of drought but because of blockade.

Broken promises are not just political—they are deeply personal. Every failed treaty, every collapsed agreement, every betrayed hope is another crack in the bridge of trust.

The Human Cost of Continuing Conflicts

The continuing conflicts of the Middle East have produced one of the greatest humanitarian crises of our time.

The **Palestinian refugee crisis**, the longest unresolved refugee situation in modern history, now includes millions born in exile.

The **Syrian civil war** displaced more than 13 million people—half of the country's pre-war population. Cities like Aleppo and Homs, once centers of culture and commerce, are reduced to rubble.

Iraq, after decades of dictatorship, foreign invasion, and insurgency, struggles with sectarian division and political fragility.

Yemen is facing famine on a catastrophic scale. Children die not from natural disasters but from human-made war and blockade.

In **Israel** and the Palestinian territories, the bridge of trust lies fractured. Failed peace accords, cycles of violence, and deep political rifts have left both peoples living in fear and uncertainty. Generations have grown up knowing more of walls and checkpoints than of dialogue and cooperation.

Behind these numbers are human stories. A father in a Syrian refugee camp teaches his children the alphabet by writing in the dirt, because books and schools are gone. A Palestinian grandmother tells her grandchildren stories of the orchard she once tended, now beyond a border wall. A Yemeni child wastes away in hunger, the victim of a war he cannot understand.

Trauma spreads silently. Studies of war-affected children in Gaza, Lebanon, and Iraq reveal high levels of PTSD, anxiety, and depression.

These children carry invisible wounds that will shape their entire lives. Worse, trauma becomes intergenerational—the pain of parents becomes the worldview of their children, locking entire societies in cycles of fear and anger.

The human cost of continuing conflict is not only measured in casualties or destroyed buildings but in dreams deferred, trust destroyed, and generations scarred.

In Israel, the bridge of trust fractured.

From its very birth in 1948, Israel carried both the exhilaration of homecoming and the agony of displacement. To one people, it was the long-promised return; to another, it was the great rupture, the Nakba. From the very first day, the bridge that might have carried two nations across their shared land began to splinter.

Each war that followed—the Six Day War of 1967, the Yom Kippur War of 1973—built temporary crossings of necessity but also deepened the canyon beneath. Israel gained territory, but not the peace it yearned for. For Palestinians, the bridge looked less like a passage and more like a wall rising before them. The occupied territories became the stark reminder of how fragile any attempt at reconciliation could be.

The Oslo Accords in the 1990s were perhaps the closest this bridge came to being rebuilt. The world watched as hands were shaken on the White House lawn, as if beams of hope had finally been laid across the divide. Yet almost as quickly as the scaffolding went up, it collapsed. Assassinations, suicide bombings, broken promises, and the relentless expansion of settlements shook the structure until it came crashing down again. Oslo's bridge remains one of the most haunting ruins of modern diplomacy—visible in memory, but impassable in reality.

Within Israel itself, the fractures multiplied. The bridge was not only between Jew and Arab, Israeli and Palestinian, but also between Jew and Jew—secular and religious, liberal and conservative, Ashkenazi and Mizrahi, nationalist and peace advocate. Each faction pulled at the planks in opposite directions, testing whether the bridge could hold under so many conflicting weights. Even when the structure stood, it trembled.

Gaza became another symbol of dismantled crossings. The withdrawal in 2005 should have opened a door to sovereignty, but instead it sealed another blockade. Rockets and reprisals turned what could have been a bridge of freedom into a battlefield of concrete walls and watchtowers. The language of coexistence was buried beneath the rubble of mistrust.

And yet, unlike the total collapse of Syria's coexistence, or Yemen's survival, Israel's bridge has never been reduced to ruins. It remains, though fractured—its supports bent, its planks uneven, but still standing in part. Moments of shared humanity keep surfacing: Arab and Jewish doctors working side by side in hospitals, joint businesses straddling contested lines, young people daring to imagine what their parents could not. These fragments glimmer like broken glass beneath the sun—reminders that a bridge, once built, is never wholly erased.

Israel's broken bridge is both the most fragile and the most visible in the region. It stands as a warning of how mistrust corrodes foundations, but also as a stubborn testament to possibility. For even in its fractured state, there are always those who gather at its edge, sketching blueprints, carrying stones, still believing that one day the crossing might yet be whole.

Why the Conflicts Continue

Why does the Middle East seem locked in endless turmoil? The reasons are many, layered, and deeply interwoven.

Colonial legacies left behind fragile states and borders that ignored ethnic, tribal, and religious realities.

Geopolitical rivalries turned the region into a chessboard for global powers—the U.S., Russia, Europe, and more recently China—each pursuing its interests.

Authoritarian regimes clung to power through repression, corruption, and fear, robbing citizens of dignity and opportunity.

Unresolved grievances, particularly the Israeli-Palestinian conflict, remain open wounds that destabilize the entire region.

Economic inequality and youth unemployment create frustration among the region's overwhelmingly young population.

Extremist groups exploit despair, offering false promises of dignity through violence.

Each of these factors sustains the cycle of conflict. The bridge is not only broken—it is repeatedly sabotaged. Every attempt to repair it faces resistance from those who profit from its collapse.

Rebuilding the Bridge

Yet the story does not end in despair. Across the Middle East, people continue to build bridges—quietly, persistently, often at great risk.

In refugee camps, teachers organize makeshift schools so children can learn despite war.

Women in Iraq and Syria lead peace dialogues, mediating between tribes and communities.

Interfaith organizations in Jordan and Egypt bring Jews, Christians, and Muslims together, proving that faith can be a force for peace.

Youth in Lebanon use music, art, and technology to create platforms for dialogue and activism.

Rebuilding a bridge requires vision, patience, and courage. It requires leaders who choose peace over power, societies that prioritize justice over revenge, and global citizens willing to stand with those who suffer.

The persistence of conflict does not erase the persistence of hope. The bridge is broken, but it can be rebuilt—stone by stone, conversation by conversation, generation by generation.

Why the Metaphor Matters

The "broken bridge" metaphor matters because it captures both the tragedy and the possibility of the Middle East.

It reminds us that what has been destroyed can also be repaired. It challenges us to see the region not only as a battlefield but as a place of connection waiting to be restored. It shifts the conversation from hopelessness to responsibility.

Faith traditions speak of bridges as paths of mercy and justice. Literature uses bridges as symbols of transformation. In the same way, this book uses the metaphor to call readers to imagine a future where the Middle East is once again a bridge between cultures, not a chasm of conflict.

A Call to the Reader

Why should someone in New York, Lagos, or Manila care about the continuing conflicts of the Middle East? Because the broken bridge affects us all.

Refugees fleeing war reshape global demographics.

Oil and energy crises ripple through global economies.

Extremism born of despair travels far beyond the region's borders.

The moral cost of ignoring human suffering diminishes us all.

The Middle East is not a distant problem. It is a mirror reflecting humanity's greatest challenges—and its greatest possibilities.

This book is therefore a call to action: to leaders, to citizens, to readers everywhere. Whether through advocacy, education, humanitarian support, or simply choosing empathy over indifference, each of us can help lay the stones of a new bridge.

The **broken bridge** is both the metaphor and the reality. It symbolizes the continuing conflicts that have defined the Middle East for generations.

This chapter has introduced the idea that these conflicts are not accidents but the result of history, politics, and human choices. They continue to this day, shaping millions of lives. But it has also introduced the conviction that the bridge, though broken, can be rebuilt.

The journey ahead will trace the roots of these conflicts, examine their global impact, and explore the possibilities for peace. The conflicts continue—but so does hope. The bridge is broken—but it is not beyond repair.

Deep Historical Context of Middle East Conflicts

The Continuity of Conflict: How the Bridge Kept Cracking

One of the most important facts that shapes life in the Middle East is the persistence of conflict. Unlike a single, contained war that ends and is followed by a period of peace, many of the region's struggles have been continuous and overlapping — a palimpsest of violence and failed fixes. New crises rarely arrive on a clean slate; they build on past ruptures, exploit unfinished grievances, and draw from the same well of unresolved injustice. To understand why the bridge remains broken, we must see how each era of conflict layered onto what came before, making repair more difficult with every cycle.

A map of the region's wars is therefore not a series of isolated islands but a braided river: boundaries of one conflict flow into another; displaced populations feed political discontent elsewhere; arms and ideologies cross borders with little regard for the artificial lines drawn on the maps. The continuity of conflict has created a living geography of trauma: communities that expect violence as normal, institutions that govern through force or patronage, and economies that are reshaped around scarcity, survival, and military spending.

In the sections that follow we trace the architecture of this continuity, beginning with the dramatic political reordering that followed the collapse of the Ottoman Empire and moving forward through the key turning points that anchor the present moment.

Colonial Legacies: Sykes–Picot, the Ottoman Collapse, and Mandates (Expanded)

The fall of the Ottoman Empire after World War I was more than the collapse of a dynasty; it was the unraveling of a centuries-old political order that had, for all its flaws, provided a framework of governance across much of the Middle East. For four hundred years, the Ottomans administered vast territories from Istanbul, balancing diverse religious and ethnic communities through the **millet system**, which allowed local autonomy under the larger imperial umbrella. This system was far from perfect, but it provided a sense of continuity: Armenians, Kurds, Arabs, Turks, Greeks, and Jews all lived within an order that recognized difference but maintained an overarching sovereignty.

When the empire crumbled under the weight of war and internal decline, the people of the Middle East expected self-determination. Arab leaders, many of whom had supported the Allied powers against the Ottomans, believed independence was their reward. In 1916, British officials even entered into correspondence with Sharif Hussein of Mecca, promising Arab independence in return for support against Ottoman rule.

The fall of the Ottoman Empire at the end of the First World War reshaped the Middle East with borders drawn in ink rather than in bloodlines, trade, or tradition. The Sykes–Picot Agreement of 1916 and the League of Nations Mandates that followed turned vast stretches of the Arab world into colonial zones of influence, binding together peoples with little shared history and dividing communities that had lived side by side for centuries. Iraq, Syria, Lebanon, and Palestine became the most visible canvases of this new order, their boundaries imposed by distant powers with little concern for the voices of those who lived within them.

Though Iran (then Persia) was never formally partitioned under Sykes–Picot, its fate was deeply entangled in the same imperial logic. Britain and Russia had already carved Iran into spheres of influence through the 1907 Anglo-Russian Convention, treating the country less as a sovereign nation and more as a buffer zone. Its borders were not redrawn on a map like Iraq or Syria, but its sovereignty was hollowed out in practice. British control over Iran's oil fields, cemented through the Anglo-Persian Oil Company, turned the country's natural wealth into a colonial asset. The Persian people lived with the paradox of formal independence but real dependency.

The collapse of the Ottoman Empire created a vacuum in which European powers sought to dominate trade routes, resources, and strategic corridors. Iran became a pawn in this geopolitical game. During both world wars, it was occupied by foreign armies—first by the British and Russians, later by the Allies, who deposed Reza Shah in 1941 to secure supply lines to the Soviet Union. Colonial fingerprints were everywhere, even if Iran was not officially labeled a mandate.

The legacy of these intrusions runs deep. The 1953 Anglo-American coup that overthrew Prime Minister Mohammad Mossadegh, after he attempted to nationalize Iran's oil, was itself a direct continuation of the colonial mindset: foreign powers deciding the fate of nations in service of their own interests. Just as Sykes–Picot and the Mandates denied Arab peoples the right to self-determination, so too did foreign intervention in Iran deny its people the chance to chart their own path.

Thus, Iran's story belongs within the same chapter of colonial legacies—not because of new borders drawn on paper, but because of sovereignty undermined, resources exploited, and political futures hijacked. While the Middle East was being divided by artificial lines, Iran was bound by invisible chains of foreign influence. These chains would fuel a century of resentment, revolution, and resistance, shaping Iran's modern posture as a nation determined never again to be carved up or controlled by outsiders.

But while these promises were being made, Britain and France were secretly negotiating the **Sykes–Picot Agreement** (1916), carving up the Ottoman domains into zones of influence. The betrayal was staggering. Instead of independence, Arabs found themselves subject to a new kind of imperialism. The Allies justified this under the League of Nations' mandate system, claiming they were "guiding" these territories to eventual self-rule. In reality, the mandates became colonial possessions by another name.

Britain took Palestine, Transjordan, and Iraq, securing control over vital oil reserves and access routes to India.

France claimed Syria and Lebanon, imposing a system that favored certain elites and fostered divisions among communities.

The Arabian Peninsula was left fragmented, with rival monarchies emerging, some supported by Britain.

These arrangements were not drawn with the peoples' aspirations in mind. They were engineered to maximize strategic advantage: securing oil, protecting trade routes, and preventing rivals from gaining influence. The map itself was often surreal: rulers in London and Paris drew straight lines across deserts, ignoring tribal affiliations, trade patterns, or historical ties. Winston Churchill, who as Colonial Secretary helped define Iraq's borders, once joked about "creating countries out of ink and a few pens."

The consequences of these decisions have echoed for a century. Artificial borders produced fragile states. Communities once linked across regions were suddenly divided into separate countries. Tribal groups found themselves split, religious minorities subordinated, and resource-rich lands claimed by newly drawn states.

Consider **Iraq**: it was stitched together from three Ottoman provinces— Basra, Baghdad, and Mosul—that had little in common culturally or politically. Sunnis, Shi'a, and Kurds were bound together in one state, governed initially by a monarch installed with British support. Unity required coercion, and the legacy of forceful rule persisted for decades, culminating in Saddam Hussein's dictatorship and the violent sectarianism that followed his fall.

Or take **Lebanon**: the French mandate encouraged a political system that institutionalized sectarian identity as the basis of politics, granting certain privileges to Maronite Christians and dividing other communities into quotas. While this system provided short-term stability, it embedded divisions into the state's DNA, eventually contributing to the eruption of Lebanon's brutal civil war (1975–1990).

The **Palestinian question** also emerged directly from the mandate era. Britain's **Balfour Declaration (1917)** had promised support for a Jewish homeland in Palestine while also pledging to protect the rights of existing Arab inhabitants. In practice, Britain struggled to reconcile these conflicting commitments. Jewish immigration increased, Arab opposition intensified, and tensions mounted. By the time Britain relinquished the mandate in 1948, the stage was set for one of the world's most enduring and painful conflicts.

Three deep legacies of the mandate period continue to fuel the Middle East's conflicts today:

Distrust of Foreign Powers. The duplicity of colonial agreements (Hussein–McMahon vs. Sykes–Picot, Balfour's ambiguity) fostered a deep suspicion of Western involvement. Even today, conspiracy theories about hidden Western agendas draw power from this historical betrayal.

Fragile, Artificial States. Borders imposed by outsiders produced states that lacked legitimacy in the eyes of many of their citizens. Internal divisions were not accidents but baked into the system. As a result, national identities often struggled to take root.

Unresolved Claims and Exclusions. From Palestine to Kurdistan, promises of self-determination were selectively applied. Groups denied recognition—Palestinians, Kurds, Armenians—became perpetual sources of grievance and resistance.

In short, the colonial legacy left behind **fractured societies, fragile states, and festering grievances**. The bridge had already cracked before the modern Middle East fully emerged. Every subsequent conflict—Arab–Israeli wars, proxy battles, civil wars—has played out on the unstable foundation laid a century ago.

The Birth of Israel and the Arab–Israeli Wars: A Continuing Fault Line

The establishment of the State of Israel in 1948 is one of the most consequential turning points in the modern history of the Middle East. To Jewish communities worldwide, it represented the long-sought dream of a homeland — a sanctuary after centuries of persecution culminating in the Holocaust. To the Arab and Palestinian populations, however, it was experienced as the **Nakba**, the "catastrophe," marked by mass displacement, dispossession, and the erasure of communities from their ancestral lands.

This duality — triumph for some, trauma for others — became the foundation for a conflict that has continued for over seven decades. The "broken bridge" metaphor is vividly embodied here: the attempt to build one community's safe haven fractured another's nationhood, and the chasm has yet to be bridged.

The 1948 War and the Nakba

When the United Nations voted in 1947 to partition Palestine into Jewish and Arab states, the plan was accepted by Zionist leaders but rejected by Arab leaders and the majority of the Palestinian Arab population. They saw the division as unjust: how could a majority Arab land, with centuries of continuous presence, be partitioned to create a Jewish state that many saw as the project of European colonialism?

Violence broke out even before the British withdrew. In 1948, when Israel declared independence, neighboring Arab states — Egypt, Jordan, Syria, Lebanon, and Iraq — invaded. The war that followed had two outcomes of lasting significance:

Israel's Survival and Expansion. Against expectations, the new state not only survived but expanded its territory beyond the UN's partition lines. For Israelis, this cemented the narrative of resilience and survival against overwhelming odds.

The Palestinian Exodus. Over **700,000 Palestinians** were displaced or fled during the fighting, many never allowed to return. Entire villages were depopulated, with some destroyed or repopulated by Jewish immigrants. Camps set up for refugees in Lebanon, Syria, Jordan, and Gaza were labeled "temporary," yet decades later, they remain, passed down to children and grandchildren.

For Israelis, 1948 is remembered as independence; for Palestinians, it is remembered as dispossession. The foundational trauma of the Nakba remains unresolved, shaping identity, politics, and grievance to this day.

The 1956 Suez Crisis

Barely a decade later, the Middle East was again engulfed in war. Egyptian President **Gamal Abdel Nasser** nationalized the Suez Canal, prompting an invasion by Britain, France, and Israel. Militarily, the invasion succeeded, but diplomatically it was a failure: under U.S. and Soviet pressure, the invading forces withdrew.

The Suez Crisis revealed two important dynamics:

The decline of European colonial powers and the rise of the U.S. and Soviet Union as the region's primary external influencers.

Israel's increasing entanglement in broader geopolitical conflicts. Its alliance with Britain and France during the crisis deepened Arab perceptions of Israel as a Western colonial implant rather than a legitimate regional actor.

The crisis also elevated Nasser as a pan-Arab hero, fueling Arab nationalism and a vision of regional unity against Israel and Western influence.

The 1967 Six-Day War

In June 1967, rising tensions exploded into a short but transformative war. Israel launched a preemptive strike against Egypt, Syria, and Jordan, defeating their forces in just six days. In the aftermath, Israel occupied:

The **Sinai Peninsula** (from Egypt)

The **Gaza Strip** (from Egypt)

The **West Bank** and **East Jerusalem** (from Jordan)

The **Golan Heights** (from Syria)

This war was pivotal. Israel's territorial expansion placed millions of Palestinians under direct Israeli military rule, intensifying grievances and embedding the conflict deeper into daily life. For Israelis, the victory was seen as miraculous — proof of military strength and divine favor. For Arabs, it was humiliating, a crushing defeat that discredited pan-Arab unity and left bitterness in its wake.

The occupation of the West Bank and Gaza, unresolved to this day, became one of the central issues of the Israeli–Palestinian conflict. Every settlement, every checkpoint, every clash since then is a continuation of that moment.

The 1973 Yom Kippur War

In October 1973, Egypt and Syria launched a surprise attack on Israel during the Jewish holy day of Yom Kippur, aiming to reclaim lost territory. Though initially successful, the offensive eventually faltered, and Israel regained the upper hand with U.S. support.

The war, however, shifted the political landscape. Egypt's determination to reclaim the Sinai paved the way for President Anwar Sadat's eventual peace initiative, leading to the **Camp David Accords (1978)** and Egypt's recognition of Israel in return for the Sinai Peninsula. This was the first peace treaty between Israel and an Arab state — a bridge of sorts rebuilt, but at a cost: Sadat's assassination in 1981 by extremists opposed to reconciliation.

The Yom Kippur War also revealed the growing global stakes. The Arab oil embargo of 1973, launched in solidarity with Egypt and Syria, shocked global markets and demonstrated how the Middle East's conflicts could ripple across the world.

Intifadas and Oslo

By the 1980s, Palestinian frustration boiled over. The First Intifada (1987–1993) was a grassroots uprising in the West Bank and Gaza, characterized by protests, strikes, and clashes with Israeli forces. It demonstrated that Palestinians would not accept indefinite occupation.

The uprising set the stage for the Oslo Accords (1993), in which Israeli and Palestinian leaders shook hands on the White House lawn, promising mutual recognition and a path toward a two-state solution. For a brief moment, the bridge seemed under reconstruction. Yet hope quickly faded. Oslo failed to resolve key issues — settlements, Jerusalem, refugees — and violence resumed with the Second Intifada (2000–2005). Suicide bombings, Israeli military responses, and deep mistrust hardened divisions further.

Oslo became, for many, another broken promise — another crack in the bridge.

A Conflict That Refuses to End

What makes the Arab–Israeli conflict such a central fault line in the Middle East is not only its persistence but its regional and global resonance. For decades, the conflict has been:

A rallying cry for Arab nationalism. Leaders from Nasser to Saddam Hussein used the Palestinian cause to legitimize their regimes.

A magnet for global intervention. The U.S., Russia, the EU, and the UN have all tried, and often failed, to broker peace.

A source of extremism. Groups like Hamas and Hezbollah, and even Al-Qaeda, have used the conflict as justification for violence.

The result is that the Israeli–Palestinian question remains not a local dispute but a central axis of Middle Eastern politics. It is a conflict that continues to shape regional identity, alliances, and wars.

The Broken Bridge Embodied

The Arab–Israeli wars embody the central theme of this book: the continuity of conflict. Every war, every intifada, every failed peace process is not a discrete episode but another fracture in the same bridge. For Palestinians, the bridge was broken by displacement and occupation. For Israelis, it is threatened by insecurity and existential fear.

Each side views its survival as incompatible with the other's justice. Until that perception is changed, the bridge will remain broken, its ruins casting long shadows over the entire Middle East.

Cold War Rivalries and Proxy Battles

When the Second World War ended, the Middle East did not become a neutral arena where emerging nations could freely experiment with self-rule and national identity. Instead, it became one of the most heavily contested theaters of the Cold War, the ideological and geopolitical struggle between the United States and the Soviet Union. Both powers saw the Middle East not simply as another region, but as a prize — a pivot point for the balance of global power.

Why? The reasons were many. The Middle East sat at the geographic crossroads of Europe, Asia, and Africa. It contained the most strategically important waterways in the world — the Suez Canal, the Bosporus, the Dardanelles, the Strait of Hormuz. Whoever influenced these chokepoints influenced the flow of oil, goods, and armies. More importantly, the region held enormous energy reserves. Middle Eastern oil had fueled Allied victory in World War II, and both Washington and Moscow understood that whoever controlled access to those reserves would hold leverage over the industrial economies of the postwar era.

Finally, the Middle East carried symbolic weight. It was the birthplace of Judaism, Christianity, and Islam, a region of spiritual resonance that drew the attention of billions worldwide. It was also the site of numerous anti-colonial struggles, and for the superpowers — one claiming to lead the "free world," the other championing global revolution — every revolution, coup, or treaty carried ideological significance.

In this way, the Cold War transformed the Middle East into a chessboard, but the pieces were not inert. Local actors — Arab nationalists, monarchs, clerics, and liberation movements — were not passive pawns but players in their own right, leveraging superpower rivalry to pursue their agendas.

Competing for Allies

The United States and the Soviet Union courted newly independent states with different offers.

The Soviet Union presented itself as the natural ally of liberation movements fighting against colonialism and Western imperialism. It supplied arms, military advisors, and technical assistance. Countries such as Egypt under Nasser, Syria, Iraq, and later Libya all drew on Soviet patronage.

The United States positioned itself as a partner for modernization and economic growth, offering loans, infrastructure projects, and security guarantees. Its closest partners included Israel, Saudi Arabia, Jordan, Turkey, and Iran under the Shah.

This competition had profound consequences. Local rulers learned to play one side against the other, securing aid, weapons, and recognition by threatening to switch allegiances. For many regimes, alignment with a superpower became a survival strategy: the U.S. or USSR could provide the money and weapons needed to suppress dissent at home.

Militarization of the Region

The Cold War left the Middle East one of the most heavily armed regions in the world.

Egypt, aligned with the Soviets after the 1950s, received **MiG fighter jets, tanks, and surface-to-air missiles**. Soviet advisors helped train Egyptian forces, and Moscow poured billions into building projects such as the Aswan High Dam.

Israel, by contrast, became a major recipient of U.S. military aid. By the 1970s, it was flying American-made F-4 Phantoms and later F-16s, giving it a decisive edge in the skies.

Iran, under Shah Mohammad Reza Pahlavi, was one of Washington's key allies, purchasing vast quantities of American weapons. By the mid-1970s, Iran's air force was one of the largest and most advanced outside of NATO.

This militarization made wars deadlier and authoritarian rulers more entrenched. Tanks and jet fighters were not just deployed against external enemies; they were also turned inward, suppressing uprisings and protests. The story repeated across the region: regimes armed to the teeth justified repression as "national defense" against external subversion.

Lebanon: A Microcosm of Proxy Conflict

Lebanon's civil war (1975–1990) demonstrated how Cold War competition deepened local fractures. Lebanon was already fragile, with its sectarian political system balancing Maronite Christians, Sunni Muslims, Shi'a Muslims, and Druze. The arrival of large numbers of Palestinian refugees and fighters after 1948 and especially after 1970 further destabilized the balance.

What began as a domestic struggle between sectarian militias quickly spiraled into a regional and global conflict:

The **United States, France, and Israel** supported Maronite Christian factions and other pro-Western groups.

The **Soviet Union and Syria** backed leftist and Palestinian factions, funneling weapons and training.

After the **Iranian Revolution in 1979**, Tehran supported the emergence of **Hezbollah**, a Shi'a militant and political movement that became one of the most powerful actors in Lebanese politics.

The result was fifteen years of bloodshed. Beirut, once called the "Paris of the Middle East," became synonymous with car bombs, kidnappings, and sniper fire. Hundreds of thousands were displaced, tens of thousands killed, and Lebanon's institutions hollowed out. The war's endurance owed much to Cold War dynamics: each time one side weakened, its patrons replenished its arsenal. In Lebanon, the Cold War was not a backdrop — it was the fuel that kept the fire burning.

Afghanistan: The Ultimate Proxy War

Though geographically on the region's periphery, Afghanistan's war in the 1980s had enormous consequences for the Middle East. When the Soviet Union invaded Afghanistan in 1979 to prop up a faltering communist government, the United States, along with Saudi Arabia and Pakistan, saw an opportunity to give Moscow its own "Vietnam."

Billions of dollars flowed to the Afghan mujahideen — guerrilla fighters resisting Soviet occupation. Weapons included advanced Stinger missiles that allowed insurgents to shoot down Soviet helicopters. The war attracted volunteers from across the Muslim world, including young radicals who later formed the backbone of Al-Qaeda.

Two legacies of the Afghan war are critical:

Militant Networks. Afghanistan became a crucible for transnational jihadist movements. Fighters forged connections, shared ideology, and gained battlefield experience that they later carried to Algeria, Egypt, Saudi Arabia, and beyond.

Normalization of Proxy Warfare. The Afghan war demonstrated that supporting armed groups abroad could be an effective, low-cost way for states to project power. This lesson was eagerly adopted by regional actors — Iran, Saudi Arabia, Turkey — and remains a central feature of Middle Eastern conflicts today.

When the Soviets withdrew in 1989, Afghanistan collapsed into civil war, but the fighters did not disappear. The "Afghan Arabs" returned to their home countries radicalized, and some turned their sights on the West. Thus, a war fought as a Cold War proxy planted seeds that would grow into the global jihadist movements of the 1990s and 2000s.

The Iranian Revolution and U.S.–Soviet Competition

The **1979 Iranian Revolution** was a geopolitical earthquake. For the United States, the loss of the Shah meant the loss of a key pillar in its Middle Eastern strategy. The subsequent hostage crisis, in which American diplomats were held in Tehran for 444 days, poisoned U.S.– Iran relations for decades.

The revolution unsettled Moscow as well. While the Soviets initially hoped the Islamic Republic might be a partner, Ayatollah Khomeini's message of Islamic revival threatened to inspire Muslim populations within the USSR's Central Asian republics. Iran charted its own independent course, rejecting both capitalism and communism.

The **Iran–Iraq War (1980–1988)** brought Cold War cynicism into sharp relief. Saddam Hussein's Iraq, fearing Iranian revolutionary influence, launched an invasion. The conflict devolved into one of the bloodiest wars of the late 20th century, with trench warfare, chemical weapons, and mass casualties.

What is striking is that both superpowers, along with European states, sold weapons to both sides at various points, seeing the war as a way to contain Iranian influence without committing their own troops. Over a million people died, yet the outside world often treated the war as a convenient stalemate. For many in the region, this reinforced the perception that foreign powers were willing to let Middle Eastern societies bleed so long as their own interests were served.

Patterns of Proxy Warfare

Across these decades, a series of patterns became entrenched:

Local conflicts became globalized. Civil wars, sectarian disputes, and nationalist struggles were drawn into the Cold War as each side sought to deny its rival influence.

Militaries became dominant political actors. Superpower aid bolstered armies, turning them into not just defenders of the state but the ruling institutions themselves. Coups and military regimes became commonplace.

Authoritarian regimes gained resilience. So long as they aligned with one superpower, they could count on weapons, money, and diplomatic cover, insulating them from domestic accountability.

Proxy warfare became normalized. Arming militias, sponsoring insurgents, and funding political movements abroad became standard tools of foreign policy.

The Cold War's End — But Not Its Effects

When the Soviet Union collapsed in 1991, many believed the world was entering a new era. In the Middle East, however, the end of the Cold War did not bring peace. The habits and structures it created — militarization, authoritarian resilience, and proxy networks — outlived the Cold War itself.

The **United States emerged as the sole superpower**, leading the Gulf War to expel Saddam Hussein from Kuwait in 1991. But Russia, though weakened, maintained its ties with Syria and later reasserted itself by intervening in the Syrian civil war in 2015. The ghosts of the Cold War still stalked the region.

The Cold War years established what might be called the **rules of dysfunction**: local grievances internationalized, regimes empowered to repress, and militias treated as permanent features of politics. The bridge of peace was not only broken; it was deliberately sabotaged by actors who saw more to gain from conflict than from reconciliation.

The Gulf Wars and State Fragility: Iraq as a Case Study

Iraq Before the Storm: A Nation of Contradictions

To understand Iraq's descent into fragility, one must first understand the paradox of the Iraqi state before its collapse. Iraq was not always synonymous with war and instability.

In the 1970s, fueled by soaring oil revenues, Iraq was seen as one of the most promising Arab states. Baghdad was cosmopolitan, a hub of intellectual and cultural life. Universities produced doctors, engineers, and scholars who were respected across the region. Women participated in public life at levels uncommon in the Middle East. The government invested in healthcare, education, and infrastructure, raising living standards.

Yet prosperity came at a price. The Ba'athist state under Saddam Hussein was deeply authoritarian. Secret police watched over daily life. Dissent was punished with torture, exile, or execution. While Iraq's outward image was one of progress, its foundations were built on coercion, fear, and militarization.

This dual reality — prosperity masking repression — helps explain why Iraq collapsed so dramatically once the storms of war arrived. The "bridge" of modernity Iraq seemed to be building was not anchored on stable ground.

The Iran–Iraq War: Scars That Never Healed

The **Iran–Iraq War** was more than just a conflict between two states. It was a clash of identities, ideologies, and ambitions. For Saddam Hussein, it was a chance to assert Iraq as the leader of the Arab world and check the spread of Iran's revolutionary Shi'a Islam. For Ayatollah Khomeini's Iran, it was a test of the endurance of the revolution itself.

The war dragged on for eight years, leaving entire border cities in ruins. The oil-rich region of **Khuzestan** in Iran and **Basra** in Iraq became wastelands of trenches, chemical attacks, and artillery barrages. Families were shattered as hundreds of thousands of young men were conscripted and sent to the front.

Saddam did not hesitate to use chemical weapons — not only against Iranian troops but also against his own Kurdish population. The infamous **Halabja massacre of 1988** saw thousands of Kurdish civilians killed with mustard gas and nerve agents, an atrocity that left lasting scars in Kurdish memory and deepened Iraq's internal fractures.

By the time the war ended in a stalemate, Iraq was heavily indebted. The economy that had once flourished in the 1970s was crumbling. Iraq's "bridge" to modern prosperity was weakened, its stones cracked under the weight of war debt and human loss.

The Gulf War: The Breaking Point

Saddam's decision to invade **Kuwait in 1990** was both reckless and revealing. Reckless, because he underestimated the international response; revealing, because it exposed the desperation of a regime drowning in debt.

When the U.S.-led coalition launched Operation Desert Storm in January 1991, the war was swift but devastating. Precision bombs struck Baghdad. Iraqi soldiers retreating from Kuwait were annihilated on the infamous **"Highway of Death"** — images of charred vehicles and bodies burned into the world's memory.

For Iraqis, the humiliation of military defeat was compounded by the aftermath: **sanctions** that crippled the economy. Ordinary citizens faced food shortages, medicine scarcity, and collapsing infrastructure. International observers reported rising child mortality rates, with UNICEF estimating hundreds of thousands of preventable deaths during the 1990s.

Yet Saddam remained in power. His regime survived not because of its strength but because sanctions, paradoxically, weakened the population more than the dictator. The Iraqi state was hollowing out, its institutions starved, its people impoverished, but its authoritarian grip intact. The bridge was breaking plank by plank.

2003 and the "Shock and Awe"

When the U.S. invaded Iraq in **March 2003**, the world watched the skies over Baghdad light up with fire as American bombs fell in the campaign dubbed **"Shock and Awe."** Saddam's forces collapsed quickly, and his regime was toppled within weeks.

But the end of Saddam was not the beginning of stability. In fact, it was the moment Iraq tipped into **state collapse**.

The **Coalition Provisional Authority's decisions** — to disband the army and purge Ba'ath Party members — dismantled the very skeleton of the state. The ministries, the bureaucracy, the police — all were gutted overnight. What remained was a vacuum, filled not by democracy but by looting, lawlessness, and insurgency.

For many Iraqis, the occupation felt less like liberation and more like humiliation. American tanks rolled through streets, foreign administrators dictated laws, and symbols of sovereignty were erased. The bridge of statehood — already cracked — was now deliberately dismantled.

Sectarianism Unleashed

The invasion unleashed forces that had long been suppressed but never resolved. Saddam's rule, brutal though it was, had kept sectarian divisions between **Shi'a, Sunni, and Kurdish communities** under tight control. Once his regime fell, these divisions erupted into open conflict.

Sunni resentment: Formerly dominant under Saddam, many Sunnis now felt excluded from the new Shi'a-led government. Insurgent groups formed, targeting both coalition forces and Shi'a civilians.

Shi'a ascendancy: Backed by Iran, Shi'a parties and militias consolidated power, seeking revenge for decades of oppression.

Kurdish autonomy: In the north, Kurds seized the moment to strengthen their semi-independent region, complete with their own government and security forces.

Baghdad became a city of walls. Neighborhoods were divided along sectarian lines, with checkpoints and concrete barriers separating communities. Car bombings and assassinations turned daily life into a gamble.

The dream of democracy had turned into a nightmare of **sectarian civil war**.

The Rise of ISIS: Fragility Becomes Collapse

The ultimate consequence of Iraq's fragility was the emergence of **ISIS**. By 2014, this extremist group swept across northern Iraq, capturing Mosul, Fallujah, and vast stretches of territory.

How could such a group rise so quickly? The answer lies in Iraq's broken state:

A hollowed-out army, rife with corruption, abandoned posts without a fight.

Sunni populations, alienated by the Shi'a-led government, saw ISIS not as liberators but as the "lesser evil" against Baghdad's neglect.

The chaos of neighboring Syria's civil war provided fertile ground for cross-border expansion.

ISIS declared a caliphate, ruling with a mix of terror, brutality, and propaganda. For Iraqis, it was yet another chapter of displacement, mass killings, and despair. Entire cities — Mosul, Tikrit, Ramadi —

were left in ruins after the fight to retake them.

Iraq's Legacy: Lessons in Fragility

Iraq's modern history is a chain of broken bridges:

The bridge of modern prosperity (1970s) shattered by dictatorship and war.

The bridge of Arab nationalism (1980s) shattered by the Iran–Iraq War.

The bridge of sovereignty (1991) shattered by sanctions and international isolation.

The bridge of democracy (2003) shattered by occupation, sectarianism, and state collapse.

The bridge of security (2010s) shattered by the rise of ISIS.

For the Iraqi people, each collapse meant another generation lost, another dream deferred. Schools destroyed, hospitals overwhelmed, families scattered as refugees — the human cost has been staggering.

And yet, Iraq endures. Protest movements in recent years — especially among youth in Baghdad and Basra — demand an end to corruption, foreign interference, and sectarianism. They wave not the flags of militias or foreign powers, but the Iraqi flag itself, reclaiming national identity.

This persistence is a reminder that even the most broken bridges can inspire efforts at rebuilding.

Why Iraq Matters

Iraq is not just a story about one nation's suffering. It is a cautionary tale for the world. It shows:

How fragile states can unravel when wars strip away institutions.

How foreign interventions, no matter how powerful, cannot engineer stability without local legitimacy.

How sectarian divisions, once politicized, can take generations to heal.

How the people, despite everything, continue to rise and demand dignity.

Iraq's broken bridge remains one of the most important case studies in modern geopolitics — a warning that war may topple regimes, but it rarely builds peace.

The Arab Spring: Hopes, Revolts, and the Return of Counter-Revolution (Heavily Expanded)

The Arab Spring was one of the most electrifying moments of the 21st century. For a brief span between late 2010 and 2012, it seemed that the political map of the Middle East and North Africa was being redrawn not by coups or foreign powers, but by ordinary people demanding dignity, justice, and freedom. Images of vast crowds filling city squares, chanting "ash-sha'b yurīd isqāṭ an-niẓām" ("the people want the fall of the regime"), reverberated far beyond the region.

For decades, Middle Eastern regimes had appeared immovable. Presidents-for-life ruled through fear, patronage, and foreign support. Citizens were accustomed to seeing elections as rubber stamps, parliaments as decorative, and police as the ultimate authority. Suddenly, in country after country, these same citizens defied the guns, the tanks, and the prisons.

But the Arab Spring was also a story of fragile institutions, fragmented oppositions, and brutal counterattacks. What began as peaceful protest cascaded into civil wars, coups, and crackdowns. It left behind a paradox: the greatest wave of political mobilization in the modern Middle East, and yet also one of its darkest legacies of repression and conflict.

The Spark in Tunisia

The story begins in **Sidi Bouzid, Tunisia**, on December 17, 2010. Mohamed Bouazizi, a young fruit seller, had long struggled to provide for his family. His small stall represented survival in a system where jobs were scarce and dignity scarcer. When municipal officials once again harassed him, confiscated his goods, and reportedly insulted him publicly, something inside him broke. In desperation, he set himself on fire outside the local governor's office.

Bouazizi's act of protest was deeply personal, but it struck a nerve. Tunisians across the country saw in him their own grievances — the daily humiliations, the corruption, the unemployment, the suffocating control of a regime that offered stability without respect. Within hours, protests erupted in Sidi Bouzid. Within days, they spread across Tunisia. By January 14, 2011, President Zine El Abidine Ben Ali — who had ruled for 23 years — fled the country.

The fall of Ben Ali proved what many had thought impossible: dictators could be toppled by the people.

Egypt: Tahrir Square and the Limits of Revolution

Tunisia's success electrified Egypt, the Arab world's most populous country and cultural hub. On January 25, 2011, tens of thousands gathered in **Cairo's Tahrir Square**, demanding the resignation of President Hosni Mubarak, who had ruled for nearly 30 years.

The protests swelled. Workers went on strike. Youth movements and Islamists, secular activists and ordinary citizens, came together in a rare moment of unity. The police state cracked, and by February 11, Mubarak resigned. The celebrations in Tahrir Square were euphoric — Egyptians believed they had reclaimed their future.

Yet Egypt's transition revealed the limits of revolutionary momentum. The country's political forces — the Muslim Brotherhood, secular liberals, leftists, and the military — did not share a common vision. In 2012, Mohamed Morsi, a Brotherhood leader, was elected president. But his government quickly alienated secular and Christian communities, while failing to address Egypt's economic crisis.

By 2013, the military reasserted control under General Abdel Fattah el-Sisi. Morsi was ousted, the Brotherhood declared a terrorist organization, and mass repression ensued. Today, Egypt is more authoritarian than it was under Mubarak, with prisons overflowing and dissent crushed. The bridge of hope built in Tahrir Square was demolished by the very institution — the military — that had pretended to be its guardian.

Libya: From Liberation to Anarchy

In Libya, protests against **Muammar Gaddafi**, who had ruled since

1969, quickly escalated into armed rebellion. Gaddafi vowed to crush dissent "house by house, alley by alley." His forces advanced on the rebel stronghold of Benghazi, threatening mass slaughter.

The international community intervened. NATO airstrikes, authorized under the banner of protecting civilians, turned the tide. By October 2011, Gaddafi was captured and killed. The revolutionaries declared victory.

Yet Libya's story did not end with liberation. The regime had been built around Gaddafi's personal rule, with no functioning institutions beneath him. When he fell, the state collapsed. Rival militias, flush with weapons, refused to disarm. Competing governments emerged in Tripoli and Tobruk. Regional powers backed rival factions, and extremist groups seized territory.

Libya became not a democracy but a fragmented battleground, a cautionary tale of how revolutions without institutions can descend into chaos.

Syria: From Protest to Apocalypse

Perhaps nowhere was the trajectory from hope to horror as stark as in **Syria**. In March 2011, small demonstrations erupted in Daraa after schoolchildren were arrested for writing anti-regime graffiti. Security forces responded with bullets. Funerals became protests, and protests spread nationwide.

Initially, Syrians demanded reforms, not regime change. But Bashar al-Assad's government chose repression over dialogue. The crackdown radicalized the opposition. By 2012, Syria had plunged into civil war.

The conflict drew in regional and global powers:

Iran and Hezbollah intervened to keep Assad in power.

Saudi Arabia, Turkey, and Qatar backed various rebel groups.

The United States and its allies supported opposition factions but hesitated to commit fully.

Russia intervened militarily in 2015, tipping the balance decisively toward Assad.

The war devastated Syria. Aleppo and Homs became ruins. Barrel bombs, chemical weapons, and sieges turned cities into graveyards. By the mid-2010s, more than half of Syria's population had been displaced — the largest refugee crisis in modern history. Out of this chaos, ISIS emerged, exploiting the vacuum to build a "caliphate" across Syria and Iraq.

Syria became a symbol of the Arab Spring's darkest outcome: a call for dignity drowned in blood, with foreign powers treating the country as a chessboard.

Yemen: From Protest to Collapse

Yemen's uprising followed a familiar pattern. Protesters filled the streets in 2011, demanding the resignation of President Ali Abdullah Saleh, who had ruled for 33 years. Saleh eventually stepped aside in 2012, replaced by his deputy, Abd-Rabbu Mansour Hadi, under a Gulf-brokered transition.

But the transition was fragile. Yemen was already fractured by tribal rivalries, southern separatism, and economic collapse. In 2014, the Houthi movement, a Shi'a group from the north, seized Sana'a. Saleh, seeking a comeback, allied with his former enemies. A Saudi-led coalition intervened in 2015, launching a devastating air campaign.

The result has been one of the world's worst humanitarian disasters. Bombings, blockades, famine, and cholera outbreaks have killed tens of thousands and left millions malnourished. The dream of 2011 — a peaceful transition to dignity and justice — dissolved into catastrophe.

Why the Arab Spring Faltered

Why did the Arab Spring, so full of promise, collapse into repression and war? Several factors stand out:

Authoritarian Resilience. Regimes that survived did so by unleashing overwhelming force, signaling they would destroy their nations rather than lose power.

Weak Institutions. In states where rulers fell, there were few functioning institutions to manage transition. Without a neutral army, strong judiciary, or cohesive bureaucracy, revolutions gave way to chaos.

Fragmented Opposition. Protest movements united around what they opposed but often lacked a shared plan for what would come next. This fragmentation allowed old elites or militaries to reassert control.

Foreign Intervention. Regional and global powers exploited uprisings to pursue their interests, turning local struggles into proxy wars.

Legacies of the Arab Spring

Despite the tragedy, the Arab Spring reshaped the region in enduring ways:

A new political consciousness. Millions of young Arabs gained experience in activism, organizing, and challenging authority.

The myth of stability shattered. Authoritarian regimes could no longer claim that their rule guaranteed calm; citizens proved they were willing to challenge the status quo.

A warning and a hope. The Arab Spring revealed both the dangers of collapse and the possibility of change. Even where uprisings failed, the memory of mass mobilization remains a warning to rulers and an inspiration to citizens.

The Broken Bridge Once Again

The Arab Spring was, in essence, an attempt to rebuild the broken bridge of the Middle East — a bridge toward dignity, justice, and accountable governance. For a moment, citizens laid new stones with their courage. But authoritarian resilience, foreign interference, and weak institutions tore it down.

The uprisings left the region not at peace but in deeper turmoil. Yet they also left behind an indelible truth: the people of the Middle East do not accept dictatorship as destiny. The bridge may be broken, but the desire to cross it remains alive.

The Spark: Tunisia's Cry for Dignity

Every great historical wave begins with a moment that seems, at first, ordinary. For the Arab Spring, that moment came in **Sidi Bouzid**, a small, dusty town in central Tunisia far from the glitter of the capital or the tourist beaches along the Mediterranean coast. On December 17, 2010, a young fruit vendor named **Mohamed Bouazizi** wheeled his cart of apples and pears into the streets, as he had done countless times before.

Bouazizi was 26 years old, the eldest son of a working-class family. His father had died when he was young, leaving him to support his mother and siblings. Like many Tunisians in the country's marginalized interior, he faced a stark reality: formal jobs were scarce, especially for young men without university degrees. Selling fruit was not a dream, but it was survival.

On that morning, municipal officials confronted him once again. Street vendors in Tunisia were often harassed for bribes or paperwork that was difficult to obtain. Witnesses said an official slapped him, spat at him, and humiliated him in front of bystanders. His cart and scales — his entire livelihood — were confiscated. This was not the first time Bouazizi had been treated this way, but something in him broke. Hours later, after pleading in vain with local authorities to have his goods returned, Bouazizi stood in front of the governor's office, poured fuel over his body, and struck a match.

The flames consumed him, but they also lit something far larger: the rage of a people who recognized themselves in his humiliation.

Why Bouazizi's Act Resonated

Bouazizi's tragedy was not unique. Across Tunisia, and indeed across the Arab world, young men and women faced the same suffocating conditions:

Unemployment and underemployment. Despite relatively high literacy rates, Tunisia's interior regions suffered double-digit unemployment, especially among the youth. Many university graduates drove taxis or sold goods informally, if they could find work at all.

Corruption and nepotism. Under President Zine El Abidine Ben Ali, opportunities often depended not on merit but on connections to the ruling elite or their business networks. The ruling family, particularly the

Trabelsis (relatives of the first lady), were notorious for monopolizing industries and demanding bribes.

Regional inequality. Tunisia's coastal cities, with their tourism and commerce, received most investment, while the interior regions were left behind. Sidi Bouzid symbolized this neglect — geographically distant from power, economically marginalized, and socially voiceless.

Loss of dignity. Perhaps most important was the erosion of karāma — dignity. To be slapped and insulted by petty officials, to live without meaningful work, to be unable to support one's family — this was not merely economic deprivation but a profound assault on self-worth.

When Bouazizi set himself ablaze, Tunisians saw their own frustrations made visible. His act spoke to something deeper than politics: the human hunger for dignity.

The Fire Spreads

News of Bouazizi's self-immolation spread rapidly. Within hours, protests broke out in Sidi Bouzid. At first, they were small gatherings — neighbors and relatives demanding justice. But social media, particularly Facebook, amplified the story. Videos of clashes with police circulated widely, reaching Tunisians across the country.

Within days, demonstrations erupted in Kasserine, Gafsa, and Sfax. Protesters were not merely asking for Bouazizi's dignity to be restored; they were demanding their own. The chants that filled the streets echoed a simple, powerful truth: *"Work, freedom, dignity!"*

The government responded with repression. Police fired live ammunition, killing demonstrators. Funerals became rallying points, each one swelling the crowds larger. Instead of quelling dissent, every act of brutality confirmed what people already believed — that the regime did not respect their lives.

By early January 2011, protests reached Tunis, the capital. Trade unions, lawyers, students, and professionals joined the movement. The uprising was no longer just about Bouazizi or unemployment — it had become a national revolt against dictatorship itself.

The Fall of Ben Ali

For 23 years, President Ben Ali had seemed immovable. He had built a police state where surveillance and repression were routine. Dissidents disappeared into prisons, journalists were silenced, and elections were stage-managed. Yet now, crowds were openly demanding his resignation.

On January 13, Ben Ali appeared on state television, promising reforms, jobs, and lower food prices. He even vowed not to run again in 2014. But it was too late. The people no longer believed him.

The next day, January 14, hundreds of thousands marched on Tunis. Under pressure from the military, Ben Ali fled the country with his family, boarding a plane to Saudi Arabia. The impossible had happened: a dictator had fallen to the power of the streets.

The Broader Meaning of Tunisia's Uprising

Tunisia's revolt was the spark that set the Arab world alight. For decades, citizens across the region had been told that dictatorships were inevitable, that Arab societies were not ready for democracy, that repression was the price of stability. Bouazizi's flames and the fall of Ben Ali shattered that illusion.

For Tunisians, the revolution marked the beginning of an ongoing experiment in democracy. Unlike in other Arab Spring countries, Tunisia managed to navigate a relatively peaceful transition. A new constitution was drafted, elections held, and a fragile but real democracy took shape. Yet challenges remained — economic stagnation, corruption, and political assassinations tested the new system. Still, Tunisia stood out as the one place where the Arab Spring's promise did not entirely collapse.

For the rest of the region, Tunisia's uprising carried two messages:

Change was possible. If Tunisians could topple their dictator, so could Egyptians, Libyans, Syrians, Yemenis, and others.

Dignity mattered. Bouazizi did not die demanding an ideology or a party program. He died demanding recognition of his humanity. That demand resonated more deeply than any abstract slogan.

A Cry That Still Echoes

More than a decade later, Tunisia still struggles with economic crisis and political turbulence, but Bouazizi's name remains etched in the consciousness of the Arab world. He has become a symbol not only of despair but of courage — a reminder that ordinary people, when pushed to the breaking point, can ignite movements that shake the foundations of power.

The lesson of Sidi Bouzid is both inspiring and sobering. Inspiring, because it showed the possibility of change. Sobering, because it revealed how fragile that change can be when confronted by entrenched interests, weak institutions, and the weight of history.

The broken bridge of the Middle East was briefly illuminated by the fire of one young man's desperate act. For a moment, people believed it could be rebuilt. But as the uprisings spread beyond Tunisia, the forces of counter-revolution, sectarianism, and foreign interference worked to ensure that the bridge would collapse once again.

21st-Century Conflicts: Syria, Yemen, Gaza, and the Regional Cascade (Fully Expanded)

The Middle East entered the 21st century with a heavy inheritance: colonial borders, authoritarian regimes, Cold War rivalries, and the unfulfilled promises of peace processes. The dawn of the new millennium should have been a chance to repair the broken bridge of the region — a chance to build on oil wealth, demographic energy, and rising global interconnectedness. Instead, it became a time when the bridge splintered further.

Three conflicts — in Syria, Yemen, and Gaza — exemplify how the old legacies combined with new crises to produce a cascade of suffering. These wars are not isolated tragedies; they are nodes in a regional web of instability. Together, they form the broken bridge of the present era: a shattered infrastructure of trust, diplomacy, and coexistence.

Syria: Revolution Drowned in Blood

When Syrians first took to the streets in March 2011, their chants were modest. "Freedom!" "Dignity!" "The people want reform!" Few called for the overthrow of President Bashar al-Assad at the start. But the brutality of the state's response changed everything. Security forces opened fire on peaceful demonstrators, arrested children, and carried out collective punishments on towns. The more the regime cracked down, the louder the calls for change became.

The Descent into War

By 2012, the situation spiraled into armed conflict. Opposition groups, some secular and nationalist, others Islamist, took up arms. The regime responded with overwhelming violence: barrel bombs dropped from helicopters, chemical weapons used on civilians, entire neighborhoods besieged and starved into submission.

Cities once known for their history and culture — **Aleppo, Homs, Damascus suburbs** — became theaters of destruction. Ancient markets were reduced to ashes, UNESCO heritage sites turned into rubble.

Regional and Global Involvement

Syria's war soon became a proxy battlefield:

Iran and Hezbollah poured in fighters, money, and arms to keep Assad in power.

Russia intervened decisively in 2015, using its air force to bomb rebel-held cities and demonstrating that Moscow was back as a Middle Eastern power.

Turkey supported opposition factions while also targeting Kurdish groups it saw as linked to separatists at home.

The United States and European allies hesitated, torn between supporting opposition groups and fearing extremist dominance. They ultimately focused on fighting **ISIS**, which emerged from the chaos.

The result was a war that was at once local, regional, and global.

Human Cost

The numbers alone tell a grim story:

More than **500,000 killed.**

Over **6 million refugees**, primarily in Turkey, Lebanon, and Jordan.

Another **6 million displaced internally**.

For many Syrians, the dream of reform had been replaced by the nightmare of statelessness. Families lived in tents in freezing winters, children grew up without schools, and entire generations knew nothing but war.

Syria represents the broken bridge in its starkest form: a once-diverse society torn apart, a nation fragmented into enclaves, a people scattered across continents.

Yemen: Starvation in the Shadow of Bombs

While Syria dominated headlines, **Yemen** descended into a disaster that the world too often ignored. Yemen had long been fragile — one of the poorest Arab states, with weak institutions, deep tribal divisions, and a history of civil wars. Yet the uprising of 2011 briefly raised hopes for change. President **Ali Abdullah Saleh**, who had ruled for over three decades, stepped aside in a negotiated transition.

From Protest to Civil War

The transition, however, quickly unraveled. Saleh never fully left the stage, maneuvering behind the scenes. The **Houthis**, a Shi'a insurgent group from the north, capitalized on grievances over corruption and neglect to seize territory. By 2014, they captured Sana'a, the capital.

Alarmed by what they saw as Iranian influence, **Saudi Arabia launched a military intervention in 2015**, leading a coalition of Arab states. Bombing campaigns devastated Yemen's cities and infrastructure. Iran, while denying heavy involvement, provided support to the Houthis, making Yemen a proxy battleground in the Saudi-Iran rivalry.

Humanitarian Collapse

The war unleashed one of the world's worst humanitarian crises:

Famine: Millions faced starvation as blockades restricted food and fuel imports. Images of skeletal children became the face of Yemen's suffering.

Disease: Cholera outbreaks infected hundreds of thousands, overwhelming what remained of the healthcare system.

Displacement: Millions fled their homes, living in makeshift camps with little aid.

Yemen became the place where the bridge to survival itself broke. Food, medicine, clean water — the most basic connections that sustain human life — were severed. Unlike in Syria, where bombs leveled cities, in Yemen hunger and disease became weapons of war.

Gaza: Living Behind the Wall

If Syria and Yemen show collapse into war, **Gaza** represents another form of the broken bridge: isolation and perpetual siege.

This small strip of land, just 140 square miles, is home to more than two million Palestinians. Since 2007, when **Hamas** took control of Gaza, it has been under blockade by Israel (and to a lesser extent Egypt). Israel argues the blockade is necessary for security, but for Gazans it has meant suffocation: restricted movement, limited imports, and economic collapse.

Cycles of Violence

Gaza has endured repeated wars:

2008–2009 ("Operation Cast Lead"): Over 1,000 Palestinians killed.

2012: Another round of rockets and airstrikes.

2014 ("Operation Protective Edge"): A 50-day war killed more than 2,000 Palestinians and left tens of thousands homeless.

2021: Eleven days of fighting killed hundreds and destroyed high-rise buildings.

Each conflict follows a grim cycle: Hamas launches rockets; Israel responds with overwhelming force; civilians bear the brunt. Ceasefires bring temporary calm, but nothing changes fundamentally.

Life Under Blockade

For Gazans, daily life is a form of slow-motion war:

Electricity is limited to a few hours per day.

Water is often undrinkable.

Hospitals struggle with shortages of medicine and equipment.

Youth unemployment hovers around 60%.

For children, this means growing up amid trauma, rubble, and hopelessness. Psychologists warn of a generation scarred by repeated wars and constant fear. Gaza is not simply a broken bridge — it is a bridge deliberately dismantled, leaving its people trapped on an island of despair.

The Regional Cascade: One Broken Bridge After Another

What links Syria, Yemen, and Gaza is not just geography but interconnection. Each conflict spills into others:

Refugees from Syria reshaped politics in Europe, fueling nationalist movements and altering global debates on migration.

Yemen's war deepened the Saudi-Iran rivalry, shaping proxy dynamics in Iraq, Syria, and Lebanon.

Gaza's suffering remains a rallying cry across the Arab and Muslim worlds, influencing regional diplomacy and unrest.

Extremist groups exploit these wars, moving fighters, weapons, and ideology across borders.

The region resembles a series of **collapsed bridges**, each one adding weight to the others. When one falls, it shakes the foundations of all.

The Broken Bridge in the 21st Century

At the heart of these wars is the book's central metaphor: the **broken bridge**.

In **Syria**, the bridge of coexistence collapsed, leaving ruins and exiles.

In **Yemen**, the bridge of survival snapped, as famine and disease spread.

In **Gaza**, the bridge of freedom was dismantled, replaced by walls and blockades.

Together, they illustrate the persistence of conflict in the Middle East. The bridge is not only broken by war but also prevented from being rebuilt by the hands of those who benefit from its destruction — regimes, militias, and outside powers.

Yet amid the devastation, there remain signs of resilience. Syrian refugees rebuild lives in Europe and Turkey. Yemeni volunteers distribute food and water despite danger. Gazan youth paint murals of hope on broken walls. These acts remind us that while the bridge is shattered, its idea still lives in the hearts of the people.

Patterns and the Mechanics of Continuity

The story of the Middle East in the twenty-first century is not just about wars and uprisings, but about the *patterns* that make those wars endure. When we step back from the dust of battles and the sound of gunfire, we notice something familiar: the same motifs appear again and again. Like echoes across deserts and mountains, the rhythms of conflict repeat themselves, shaping lives from one generation to the next. These patterns are the broken beams and twisted planks of the bridge we have been describing. To understand why peace has been so elusive, we must walk across this shattered structure and examine the pieces that keep falling apart.

Fragmented Sovereignty: The Vanishing State

In the outskirts of Mosul, long after the U.S. invasion of Iraq in 2003, a woman named Layla sat outside her ruined home. The government offices in her district had been burned down years ago. The local police had disappeared. Who collected taxes? A militia. Who settled disputes? A local commander, whose word carried more weight than any judge's decree. Who protected her family when thieves came at night? Certainly not the absent state, but a group of armed men who promised safety for a monthly "contribution."

Layla's story is not unique. Across the region, ordinary people found themselves living in countries where the government existed only on paper. In Libya, after Gaddafi's fall, rival militias divided Tripoli into armed fiefdoms. In Yemen, ministries stood empty while Houthi rebels and tribal leaders ran checkpoints. The state — the bridge that should connect citizens to institutions of justice, health, and order — simply vanished.

This is how sovereignty fragments. The bridge crumbles not in one dramatic collapse, but in slow decay, until people realize that to cross it is to step into a void. And so they build smaller, makeshift bridges — militias, warlords, neighborhood councils — fragile substitutes that provide survival but no stability.

External Patronage: Wars Kept Alive from Afar

If local leaders and militias are one side of the story, foreign patrons are the other. Consider the war in Syria: what began as peaceful protests became a theater of global rivalry. Russia flew in warplanes to protect Bashar al-Assad. Iran sent militias across the border. Saudi Arabia and Turkey armed different rebel factions. The United States, too, played its part, backing Kurdish fighters against ISIS. Each external actor believed they were playing chess, but for Syrians on the ground, it felt like being trapped on the board as pawns.

The same pattern played out in Yemen, where the conflict between Houthis and the government became a proxy war between Saudi Arabia and Iran. Bombs fell not because Yemenis demanded them, but because distant powers saw strategic advantage in prolonging the fight.

Here, too, the bridge image helps us understand: every time locals tried to lay new planks of dialogue or reconciliation, foreign hands pulled them away, replacing them with weapons and suspicion. Instead of helping people cross, external patrons dynamited the foundations, ensuring that no one could reach the other side.

Identity Weaponized: Neighbors into Enemies

In a small village outside Aleppo, a grocer once sold bread and olives to families of every background: Sunni, Christian, Alawite. They greeted each other with warmth, shared weddings and festivals, and raised their children side by side. But as Syria's war deepened, armed men appeared in the village, whispering that the other community could not be trusted. Rumors spread. Old grievances, half-forgotten, were sharpened into knives. Within months, neighbors who had once shared food no longer dared walk past each other's homes.

This is how identity is weaponized. Leaders, desperate to hold power, paint politics as a struggle between "us" and "them." Saddam Hussein once wrapped himself in Arab nationalism to rally support against Iran. Bashar al-Assad cast himself as protector of minorities, while rebels framed their fight as liberation for the Sunni majority. In Yemen, sectarian rhetoric turned political disagreements into existential struggles.

When identity is twisted into a weapon, the bridge between communities does not just break — it becomes a battlefield. The very planks that once connected families are repurposed as barricades, dividing one group from another.

Economics and Youth: A Generation in Waiting

Imagine being twenty years old in Gaza. You have never known a day without blockade. You wake each morning to the hum of generators, the silence of unemployment, and the heavy question: *What future is there for me?* Sixty percent of young people in Gaza are jobless. They study, they dream, but the gates remain locked.

Across the Middle East, millions of young men and women face the same reality. In Tunisia, frustration over corruption and joblessness led a young street vendor, Mohamed Bouazizi, to set himself on fire — an act that ignited the Arab Spring. In Iraq, jobless youth join militias not out of ideology, but because they offer salaries and status. "Better a gun than an empty hand," one young man told an aid worker.

When economies fail to provide dignity, armed groups step in as employers. They offer not just money but a sense of belonging. The bridge to prosperity, which should carry youth into adulthood with purpose and pride, collapses, leaving them stranded on the side of despair. Militias and extremist groups then build their own false bridges, promising meaning through violence.

The Environment: Scarcity as a Hidden Enemy

While bombs and bullets dominate headlines, another enemy gnaws quietly at the region: scarcity. Between 2006 and 2010, Syria endured one of its worst droughts in modern history. Crops failed. Villages emptied. Families poured into cities like Damascus and Aleppo, searching for work and water. Their arrival strained already weak infrastructures, and when protests began in 2011, many of those who joined came from communities displaced by drought.

Water scarcity in Iraq fuels tensions between farmers. In Yemen, dried wells and empty cisterns drive desperate families into the arms of militias who control access to water trucks. Environmental stress acts like a silent hammer, weakening the bridge from below, until one day the whole structure gives way.

Failures of Reconciliation: Peace Without Justice

Finally, even when wars end, the region struggles to keep the peace. In Lebanon, the Taif Agreement of 1989 stopped the fighting but locked politics into sectarian quotas that ensured paralysis. In Iraq, the exclusion of Sunnis after Saddam's fall created bitterness that later fed ISIS. Again and again, peace was signed on paper but never lived on the ground.

Without accountability, warlords become ministers. Without inclusion, communities remain marginalized. Without justice, wounds fester. These failures do not mend the bridge; they build flimsy scaffolds that collapse at the first gust of crisis.

The Mechanics of Continuity: Why the Bridge Keeps Breaking

Taken together, these stories reveal the mechanics of continuity. States collapse, militias rise. Foreign powers intervene, conflicts stretch on. Identities are twisted, neighbors become enemies. Youth are denied futures, and so they seek meaning in militias. Scarcity drives desperation. Peace agreements without justice pave the way for the next war.

The broken bridge is not a single event; it is the result of these mechanisms repeating, grinding, feeding one another. The Middle East's tragedies are not inevitable — they are produced by systems that reward violence and neglect peace.

And yet, naming these patterns also reveals a path forward. If sovereignty can be rebuilt inclusively, if foreign patrons can be restrained, if economies can give dignity to youth, if water and land can be shared, if justice can be pursued honestly — then the bridge can begin to be rebuilt.

Until then, the region remains caught in continuity, walking the ruins of a bridge that has collapsed too many times to count.

The everyday politics of living in limbo

A vignette helps. Jamal (composite), a Syrian teacher before 2011, now works in a garment factory in Amman. He spends his evenings helping Syrian children with math in a makeshift school, and his days worrying about rent. He lost two brothers in the fighting. He cannot return to his neighborhood in Aleppo — neither the streets nor the memories remain intact. Yet he cannot feel truly at home in Jordan either: work permits are hard to obtain, public services are limited, and the future seems to belong only to those with citizenship.

These micro-realities add up. Refugees strain host-country services: clinics see longer queues, classrooms expand beyond capacity, housing prices climb as demand increases. Local communities—already often economically fragile—perceive competition for jobs and resources. Where policy is absent or punitive, tensions harden into resentment. Where policy allows inclusion — work permits, access to education, pathways to residency — refugees sometimes become integrated contributors to their new cities. Both outcomes are possible; the direction often depends on law, money, and politics.

For those in camps, the social fabric is altered. Refugee societies develop their own forms of authority: camp committees, youth councils, informal justice systems. Young men and women create pop-up economies: bakeries inside tents, tailoring workshops, digital call centers run from containers. But the permanency of tents produces a strange time: an entire generation grows up with a childhood in scenes of transience yet finds adulthood anchored in a fixed limbo. The sense of rootlessness becomes a political resource — for militants who promise restoration by force, or for diasporas who fund partisan politics back home.

Diaspora: identity, remittances, and politics

Displacement does not end at borders. It produces diasporas — communities scattered across the globe that carry memory, trauma, hope, and political claims with them. Diasporas are both reservoirs of suffering and engines of influence. They send money home; they lobby parliaments; they vote in host-country elections that, in some cases, shape foreign policies toward their homeland.

Consider the ways diasporas matter:

Economic lifelines. For many households, remittances from relatives abroad are the difference between survival and starvation. Syrian and Iraqi families have relied on transfers from relatives in Europe, North America, and the Gulf. Palestinian diaspora networks historically channeled funds that supported camps, social services, and political organizations. These financial flows keep societies afloat, but they also introduce dependencies and power dynamics: who controls the money shapes local politics.

Political influence. Diasporas organize politically. They fund lobbying groups, stage demonstrations, and influence media narratives. After 1948, Palestinian organizations throughout the world helped internationalize their cause; decades later, Syrian and Yemeni expatriates have used social media and advocacy to influence asylum policies and humanitarian responses. Diaspora voting and lobbying can nudge foreign governments toward intervention or aid, and sometimes toward policies that harden conflict rather than resolve it.

Transnational networks for conflict. The diaspora is not always a liberalizing force. Its bonds can mobilize funds, fighters, or political pressure that prolongs conflict. A remittance can feed a household; it can also be taxed by armed groups to fund militias. A diaspora organization can help rehabilitate a city or lobby for military intervention. The line between humanitarian support and political mobilization is thin, and wars exploit that ambiguity.

In other words, the diaspora turns displacement into a transnational geography: the battlefield extends into foreign living rooms, voting booths, and money transfer kiosks. The bridge is not only broken locally; its pieces are carried across continents where they continue to shape politics.

Cities transformed: urban demography and the remapping of daily life

Refugee flows do not only fill camps. Increasingly, displaced people move into cities — informal settlements, peripheral neighborhoods, and crowded apartments. Beirut's neighborhoods, Amman's outskirts, Istanbul's suburbs, and the tented peripheries of many Gulf cities bear the imprint of repeated waves of migration. Urban demographics change: new languages appear on shop signs; markets sell unfamiliar spices; school enrollments spike.

These changes can be enriching. Urban diversity can revitalize economies: refugee entrepreneurs open restaurants, repair shops, and small factories. Skilled migrants contribute to health and education sectors. Over time, cities can absorb and adopt newcomers, making them part of a metropolitan tapestry.

But inclusion is politically fraught. Urban hosts may resent newcomers who compete for informal jobs. Local politicians can exploit these tensions, turning refugees into scapegoats for broader economic problems. Tensions over housing, public transport, and schooling can spur xenophobic rhetoric. Urban planning rarely anticipates mass arrivals, and the resulting improvisation often leaves both host and refugee populations worse off.

From the viewpoint of the broken bridge, cities become islands of partial repair — places where new crossing points are created alongside barriers. Some bridges form: markets where Syrians and Jordanians trade; cultural festivals that bring communities together. Other bridges are replaced by tolls and checkpoints: gated neighborhoods, school quotas, and labor restrictions that keep integration shallow and fragile.

Legal limbo and the politics of rights

The experience of displacement is shaped by law. Legal status — refugee, asylum-seeker, undocumented migrant, or stateless person — matters. It determines access to work, healthcare, education, and political voice.

It also shapes dignity: to be "registered" and recognized is to be seen as human in the eyes of international law.

Two legal frameworks matter in the Middle East. Most refugees elsewhere fall under the protection of UNHCR, whose 1951 Refugee Convention defines rights and responsibilities; Palestinian refugees, however, are in large part served by **UNRWA**, an agency created specifically for them and whose mandate is distinct and politically contested. This difference in institutions creates different experiences and politics. Palestinian camps have long had their own social services and institutions — but also the burden of protracted statelessness. Syrian refugees often face varying national laws: in some countries they can work, in others they cannot.

Legal exclusion promotes informal economies and exploitation. Without the right to work, many refugees accept underpaid and precarious labor. Without access to legal residence, families live in fear of arrest, deportation, or exploitation. Statelessness — when a person lacks any recognized nationality — freezes lives in a particularly cruel stasis: no school enrollment, no passport, no legal employment.

For the broken bridge, legal limbo prevents repair. Bridges require legal recognition — rights that allow movement, work, and civic participation. When legal systems exclude displaced people, they are effectively building walls rather than pathways.

Cultural memory and the politics of return

Displacement stamps itself on memory. Songs are rewritten; cuisine carries recipes from lost orchards; children grow up with stories of home that become legendary. Cultural life in camps can be rich: theater groups, poetry circles, and schools transmit identity to younger generations. But cultural memory can harden politics. When the imperative becomes "return at any cost," compromise is hard to find. The right of return, restitution for lost property, and collective memory of dispossession are potent forces in peace negotiations — forces that sometimes make negotiated settlement more difficult because they are, rightly, non-negotiable for displaced communities.

Diaspora communities also cultivate memory: memorials, museums, and annual commemorations keep causes alive. This cultural transmission is a resource for identity, solidarity, and survival. It is also a source of political leverage that can either nudge reconciliation or entrench maximalist positions that stall compromise.

Displacement as a generator of new conflict dynamics

It is important to see displacement as not merely an effect of war but as an active generator of new conflict dynamics. How does that happen?

New recruit pools. Displaced youth with few prospects are often attractive recruits for militias and extremist groups. The experience of humiliation, loss, and a sense that the world has abandoned them makes the promise of belonging and purpose a powerful lure.

Economic engines for armed groups. Refugee economies produce opportunities for taxation, smuggling, and control that armed actors exploit. Control a border crossing or a camp market, and you can collect fees.

Polarization in host states. Refugee presence can become a domestic political issue, exploited by populists who argue for closing borders. Host governments may restrict rights in response, which can create humanitarian crises with the potential to spill back across borders.

Diaspora-financed politics. Remittances may fund social welfare — or they may flow through political networks that support armed factions. Diaspora activism can internationalize a conflict, pushing for foreign interventions or sanctions that entrench positions.

Each refugee family thus becomes part of a broader circuitry of conflict — economically, socially, and politically integrated into patterns that can reproduce violence.

Stories of resilience: refugees as agents, not only victims

To tell this story only as tragedy would be incomplete. Displacement also produces astonishing resilience. A Syrian mother starts a sewing cooperative in a Jordanian suburb, employing other refugee women and producing clothing sold online. An Iraqi physician in Detroit organizes telemedicine consultations for relatives back home and trains local clinicians in trauma care. Palestinian artists in diaspora create exhibitions that humanize a complex political story to foreign publics.

Refugees build schools, found NGOs, and lobby for improved services in their host cities.

These acts of agency matter. They create new networks of solidarity that cross borders; they build bridges of a different kind — from exile to host society, from victimhood to contribution. Such bridges are fragile and chronically underfunded, but they are crucial starting points for longer-term integration and eventual reconciliation.

Toward bridges that hold: practical pathways

If the human geography of continuity maps how displacement shapes conflict, then policy must be measured against whether it repairs or deepens those ruptures. A few principles emerge from on-the-ground experience:

Protect legal status and rights. Granting work permits, access to education, and legal residency lowers tensions and transforms refugees into contributors rather than burdens.

Invest in host communities as well as refugees. Building schools, clinics, and water systems for both host and refugee populations reduces competition and builds shared infrastructure.

Support diaspora engagement for peace. Create channels for diaspora remittances to fund development and reconciliation projects rather than militarized agendas; encourage diaspora participation in post-conflict reconstruction with accountability.

Plan for return with dignity, not as a slogan. Return requires security guarantees, property restitution, and long-term investment. "Return at any cost" is not a path to stability; neither is permanent statelessness.

Rebuild civic bridges. Support mixed civic initiatives — neighborhood committees, joint schools, interfaith councils — that rebuild trust across communities.

Address mental health and education. Trauma-informed schooling and community mental health services are long-term investments that prevent generational cycles of violence.

Each of these measures is not merely technical; it is ethical. They ask host countries, donors, and international institutions to see displaced people not as temporary burdens but as human beings with rights, agency, and potential.

Closing: Diaspora, displacement, and the shape of the broken bridge

Walk the lanes of a refugee camp at dusk and listen to the stories. You will hear of lost orchards and old weddings, of children learning two languages and of elders who refuse to forget place names. You will see economies adapted to liminal life — tent shops, bartered goods, messages sent home via mobile phones. You will also see politics in everything: who gets a water truck, which committee decides school hours, what remittances choose to fund.

Displacement remaps the Middle East. It redraws cities and shifts voting blocs, it changes economies and rearranges loyalties. In this way, the bridge of the region does not merely lie in ruins — it becomes a scattered archipelago whose pieces are carried everywhere. Sometimes those pieces are used to build peace across oceans; far too often, however, they are used to sustain conflict.

If the book's main idea is that the bridge is broken and that conflict continues as a system, then displacement and diaspora are two of the bridge's most telling, most consequential broken planks. They are evidence of rupture and channels of continuity. They are also, if policy and compassion can reshape incentives, sources of repair: human capital mobilized for reconstruction, diaspora funds channeled into schools not weapons, host-city integration programs that sow social cohesion.

Umm Salma's grandchildren grew up learning two songs — one about the olive trees she had known, another about the streetlights of the city that had adopted them. Both songs tell the same truth: people carry home in their mouths. If we are to rebuild the bridge, we must start by listening to those songs and building a world in which their children can cross a stable bridge rather than be forced to walk forever on its broken stones.

Conclusion — The Bridge as a Timeline of Unrepaired Damage

If you stand at the broken end of an old bridge and look across the gap, you can measure the damage plank by plank. You see splintered timbers, a snapped cable, rusted bolts. You can count the losses: the missing railing where a child once leaned; the stonework blackened where fire ate through a beam. Now imagine that every split timber tells a story — of an insult, a failed treaty, a blocked road, a famine, or a bombing raid. Walk that bridge from end to end and you have, in miniature, the modern history of the Middle East: a timeline not of single catastrophes but of cumulative, compounding damage.

That image — the bridge as timeline — is the central truth we have tried to put into words in this first part of the book. The Middle East did not become a landscape of ruined connections overnight. The cracks were made, widened, and rarely repaired. Borders drawn by distant hands, loyalties weaponized by desperate leaders, loans given as leverage in a proxy war, a drought that emptied villages, a promised reform that never arrived — each event is a missing plank. Each one alone might have been bridged. Taken together, they created the yawning chasm we see today.

To see how deep the damage runs, imagine returning to the bridge with a notebook and a team of builders. You would need to log not just the visible breaks but their causes: where the foundations were undermined; where rot set in because maintenance was never funded; where the bridge was deliberately attacked by those who profited from blockade and conflict. That meticulous inventory is what this chapter has been: a mapped account of how colonial cartography, Cold War rivalries, authoritarian holdovers, economic exclusion, environmental stress, and cycles of retribution accumulated into structural fragility.

Damage is cumulative because its causes reproduce themselves

What makes the Middle East's condition especially stubborn is not only the severity of each disaster but the way one failure sows the seeds for the next. Artificial borders created states with fragile legitimacy; fragile states invited foreign patrons who supplied arms and strengthened rulers who relied on repression; repression bred uprisings that were sometimes crushed and sometimes spiraled into civil war; civil war produced refugees and diasporas that, in turn, reconfigured politics beyond the battlefield; displaced youth with no prospects were ripe for recruitment by armed groups; environmental shocks pushed farmers into cities already strained by poverty — and so on.

This is not a cycle of fate; it is a set of **reproducible mechanics**. Knowing this matters because causes can be addressed. If the bridge keeps breaking because the same engines keep running — external patronage, exclusionary politics, unregulated arms flows, and economic despair — then stopping those engines is the only way to make repair possible.

Repair must be holistic — not cosmetic

Any craftsman will tell you: you cannot fix a fractured bridge with paint and good wishes. You must mend the foundation, replace load-bearing elements, re-tension the cables, and redesign vulnerable stretches so they do not fail at the next storm. So it is with nations.

"Repair" in the Middle Eastern context cannot be rhetorical. It must be structural, long-term, and sequenced. Here are the elements that, taken together, form a practical architecture for rebuilding — a blueprint, not a quick checklist:

Humanitarian triage and durable relief

Before any structural work, people must be safe and nourished. Emergency medical care, food, water, and shelter are the short-term scaffolding without which reconstruction is impossible. But humanitarian aid must be organized to avoid creating perverse incentives: it should be predictable, tied to transparent delivery mechanisms, and designed to strengthen — not supplant — local capacities.

Stabilization and protection of civilians

A credible security environment is essential for institutions to operate. This may require neutral peacekeeping forces or internationally monitored ceasefires as temporary measures. Yet stabilization cannot last forever. It must have a timetable and handover plan to locally legitimate security institutions that are accountable and inclusive.

Institution-building and state renewal

The most durable bridges rest on sound foundations: impartial courts, functioning civil services, local administrations, and accountable security forces. Rebuilding these institutions is painstaking work. It requires inclusive recruitment, meritocratic processes, training, and anti-corruption safeguards. It also requires decentralization where appropriate — empowering municipalities to manage water, schooling, and local policing so the distant capital does not remain the only actor capable of delivering basic services.

Transitional justice, truth, and reconciliation

Bridges cannot be rebuilt where memory is denied. Truth-telling processes — from local community hearings to national truth commissions — must address trauma openly. Where crimes warrant prosecution, fair trials must be held. Where communities need restitution, property returns and reparations must be executed. Justice is not merely punitive; it is part of reweaving the social fabric.

Economic recovery that centers dignity and jobs

Reconstruction cannot be purely top-down. People need livelihoods. Public works (roads, schools, water systems) can be prioritized as labor-intensive programs that employ local populations immediately after conflict. Microfinance, vocational training, support for small and medium enterprises, and incentives for private-sector investment tied to transparency can create sustainable employment. Critically, youth employment must be a central objective — not an afterthought — because disenfranchised youth are the main recruitment pool for destabilizing actors.

Environmental repair and resource diplomacy

Water scarcity, degraded soils, and climate shocks are slow-moving but powerful agents of instability. Programmes for drought resilience, basin-level water agreements, and shared infrastructure (e.g., joint desalination, wastewater recycling) turn scarcity from a source of competition into an opportunity for cooperation. Managing resources collectively builds interdependence — a practical mechanism for peace.

Demobilization, reintegration, and security-sector reform

Combatants must be offered credible alternatives: training, jobs, community service, psychological support, and legal protections for those who disarm. Security forces must be reformed with vetting, civilian oversight, and professional training. Mixing international standards with local legitimacy is the delicate art of creating forces that protect citizens rather than predate upon them.

Political inclusion and constitutional engineering

Power-sharing arrangements must be designed to gradually normalize politics rather than freeze identity divisions forever. Constitutions and electoral systems can be engineered to incentivize cross-cutting coalitions, rather than enshrine perpetual sectarian quotas. Sunset clauses, decentralization, and staggered devolution of power are technical but powerful design choices.

Regional diplomacy to remove external incentives for conflict

No national settlement will last if regional patrons profit from instability. Diplomatic backchannels must aim to constrain proxy support, establish transparency over arms flows, and offer patrons alternative means of influence — economic partnerships, trade incentives, and shared security frameworks — that make sponsorship of violence costly rather than profitable.

Diaspora engagement and refugee policy

Diasporas are not merely sources of trauma; they are reservoirs of capital, skills, and political leverage. Harnessing remittances for reconstruction (with safeguards to prevent militarization), enabling safe and dignified returns, and crafting integration policies for refugees that allow them to contribute to host economies are part of a humane, pragmatic repair strategy.

Each of these elements is necessary but not sufficient alone. They must be sequenced. Humanitarian relief buys the time for stabilization; stabilization enables institution-building; institutions make reconciliation credible; reconciliation clears the social space for economic investment. It is patient work. There are no shortcuts.

Story: a hypothetical repair in three acts

To see how this might play out, imagine a Syrian provincial city after a ceasefire. Act One: basic services are restored — water flows again, a field clinic opens, and an international monitoring force secures key thoroughfares while local councils are empowered to run markets. Act Two: a large, transparent cash-for-work program rehabilitates rubble, hiring local youth and providing vocational training. A truth and memory project begins, with community hearings that combine local elders and independent commissioners. Act Three: municipal elections, supervised and staggered to ensure representation, create a local governing coalition that partners with private investors to reopen factories. Diaspora funders match local investments. Over five to ten years, the city shifts from emergencies to normalcy. This is not miraculous; it is painstaking reversal of the mechanics that produced rupture.

The moral architecture of repair

Technical fixes require moral clarity. Repair is not merely rebuilding concrete; it is about restoring dignity. Justice must not be instrumentalized. Aid must not be misdirected to prop up spoilers. International actors must resist the facile temptation to treat reconstruction as a short-term project with political metrics; true rebuilding will take decades. Yet the moral imperative is clear: those whose actions created or profited from the breakage must be held to standards that prevent recurrence.

Hope without naïveté

It would be dishonest to promise quick fixes. The Middle East's bridge has been broken repeatedly because a constellation of powerful interests — local, regional, and global — have benefited from its fracture. Some actors will resist repair. Some communities will mistrust offers of aid. Some transitional justice measures will reopen wounds. Yet history is not only a record of destruction. South Africa, Rwanda, and Northern Ireland — each in their own imperfect way — teach that societies can move from atrocity to coexistence if citizens, leaders, and international partners commit to deep, honest work. Those examples will be the subject of later chapters, not as templates to copy, but as sources of practical learning about sequencing, truth, and the place of civil society — especially women and youth — in healing.

A final, practical covenant: local ownership and measured international help

If there is a single principle that must guide every intervention it is **local**

ownership. Repair that is seen as imposed from outside rarely endures. External actors must be honest brokers, not architects of imposed solutions. They should support local capacity, provide technical and financial tools, and leverage diplomatic influence to constrain spoilers. Measured international support — patient funding, conditional debt relief, technical expertise, and arms-control — can make the difference between reconstruction that endures and a pyrrhic reconstruction that collapses with the first relapse.

Closing the chapter and opening the work ahead

The bridge's broken planks are now mapped in our minds. We have traced how colonial decisions, Cold War rivalries, authoritarian survival tactics, the Arab Spring's tragic arcs, the wreckage of Iraq and Syria, the famine in Yemen, and the siege of Gaza have accumulated into chronic, self-reinforcing fragility. We have seen how displacement and diaspora have both borne witness and become active agents in the continuation of conflict. We have named the mechanics that keep the bridge from being mended.

Recognizing continuity is not an argument for despair. It is a call for specificity, patience, and moral courage. The remainder of this book will move from diagnosis to design. We will study peacebuilding models that have restored fractured societies elsewhere; we will look at the roles youth and women must play as agents of renewal; we will outline concrete economic strategies and environmental cooperation plans that can sustain peace; and we will propose policy packages that combine local legitimacy with international support. Each proposed repair will be grounded in case studies and practical steps, because a rebuilt bridge requires not only vision but craft.

Turn the page with the knowledge that the work ahead will be long and exacting — but possible. The bridge is broken: that is the tragedy. The knowledge that humans have rebuilt broken bridges across histories and oceans — and the evidence that ordinary people still reach across divides in the Middle East every day — is the reason this book is written. The next chapters will show not only how the bridge was broken, in fuller historical detail, but how its stones might yet be gathered and reset, so that future generations can walk across, not around, the chasm.

CHAPTER 2

International Dimensions

The Role of the United States: Peace Broker or Interventionist?

If the Middle East's modern history were a bridge, the United States would be one of the largest hands on either side — sometimes steadying the span, sometimes, whether by miscalculation or will, prying out a plank. Walking the length of that bridge, you feel the impressions of Washington everywhere: the oil contracts signed in desert palaces, the embassy flags, the aid envelopes, the battalions offloaded at ports, the diplomats pacing conference rooms. For more than seven decades, America's presence has shaped whether the bridge leaned toward crossing or collapse. That ambivalence — builder and breaker, ally and occupier, mediator and missile-launcher — is the central drama of U.S. policy in the Middle East.

This chapter tells that story as a sequence of decisions, turning points, and human consequences. It moves between rooms of diplomacy and the ruins of war, between presidential handshakes and the long lines at refugee registration centers. Throughout, the broken-bridge metaphor will be our guide: how each American action either tried to join the gap or, disastrously, widened it.

The Long Entrance: Oil, Containment, and the Cold War

Washington's deep involvement in the Middle East accelerated after World War II. Europe's empires were in retreat, and new nation-states emerged across the region. Two immediate strategic interests pushed the United States into sustained engagement.

First was **energy**. The industrial order that underpinned American power depended on reliable crude supplies. Saudi Arabia, Kuwait, Iraq, Iran — the Gulf's oilfields were not abstract resources; they were the pipelines of geopolitics. U.S. policy-makers learned early that instability in the Gulf could ripple outward, threatening global markets and American allies.

Second was **ideology** and containment. The Truman Doctrine and the logic of the early Cold War treated the Middle East as an arena where Soviet influence had to be checked. Military sales, economic aid, and political alignment became instruments to keep states from leaning toward Moscow. The net result was long-term entanglement: alliances with monarchies like Saudi Arabia and with states that could be useful against Soviet expansion, even when those partners were far from democratic.

At the grassroots this produced a paradox: American dollars and military backing often underwrote regimes that delivered oil and order, but little political space. That bargain — security in exchange for acquiescence — built modern infrastructures but hollowed civic life. In our bridge metaphor, the U.S. laid down long, well-engineered beams of security cooperation while neglecting the slow work of building social trust across communities.

The Peace-Broker Moment: Camp David and the Promise of Diplomacy

There have been moments when U.S. power looked most like a bridge-builder. The image is evergreen: a president troubling over maps, a quiet presidential retreat, two foreign leaders brought together under tight security and tutored rhetoric. Camp David in 1978 was one such moment. President Jimmy Carter, after long nights of mediation, coaxed a peace treaty from Egypt's Anwar Sadat and Israel's Menachem Begin — the first formal peace between Israel and an Arab state in the modern era. The resulting framework ended a state of war between Cairo and Jerusalem and reshaped regional calculations. The accords were not a comprehensive solution — Palestinians remained outside the final settlement — but they were proof that American diplomacy, when sustained, could form a durable crossing over deep enmities.
Office of the Historian

Two notes temper that success. First, Camp David's peace was a bilateral fix: it solved a specific interstate problem without resolving the deeper communal grievances that continued to fester. Second, success required a particular alignment of personalities and timing: leaders willing to take domestic risks and a sustained presidential focus. In short, bridge-building is possible, but it requires much more than speeches.

Oslo: A Handshake That Cut Both Ways

Fifteen years later, the world watched another American-brokered moment with near-religious hope. The **Oslo Accords** of 1993 — a handshake on the White House lawn between Yitzhak Rabin and Yasser Arafat under President Bill Clinton's smile — seemed to open a pathway for Israelis and Palestinians to walk toward a future of two states. For many observers it was the moment the broken bridge might finally be repaired. **Office of the Historian**

Yet the story of Oslo shows how fragile the work of repair can be. The accords were interim arrangements, not a final settlement; they left core issues — borders, Jerusalem, refugees — unresolved. Meanwhile, the settlement enterprise in the occupied territories continued apace, eroding Palestinian trust. Violence and political assassinations punctured the fragile optimism. The U.S., as sponsor, had leverage but increasingly found itself blamed by Palestinians for not enforcing halts to settlement expansion and by Israelis for not ensuring security. Oslo's collapse is an object lesson: high-profile diplomacy can create bridges — but without durable accountability, the bridge may carry people only a short distance before it fractures again.

The Interventionist Turn: Gulf War, Iraq 2003, and the Price of Overreach

The United States' role as a guarantor of regional order became more complicated when the instrument of policy shifted from negotiation to force. In 1990–1991, Washington led a broad coalition to eject Saddam Hussein's forces from Kuwait after Iraq's invasion. That campaign, sanctioned by the UN and seen by many as a legitimate act of collective security, reinforced the image of the U.S. as a power willing to use force to defend international norms. The legal basis — UN Security Council Resolution 678 — gave the Gulf War an aura of multilateral legitimacy. <u>Digital Library</u>

The rupture came in 2003. The U.S.-led invasion of Iraq, justified publicly by claims that Baghdad possessed weapons of mass destruction, removed a brutal dictator but also disassembled the scaffolding of statehood. The post-invasion decisions — most notably the disbanding of Iraq's military and the de-Ba'athification of its bureaucracy — left a vacuum. Ministries, courts, and municipal services collapsed; thousands of armed, unemployed men roamed cities and towns; sectarian violence escalated. The long-term consequences were catastrophic. When later inquiries examined the intelligence claims that had bolstered the case for war, the Iraq Survey Group concluded that the WMD picture had been dramatically overstated and that the prewar intelligence assessments were deeply flawed. The result was a profound erosion of U.S. credibility in the region and a landscape in which extremist groups could take root. <u>GovInfo</u>

Several consequences flow from the invasion's aftermath. First, the use of force without a robust, legitimate plan for post-conflict governance can produce state collapse rather than liberation. Second, the moral authority America claimed — to liberate peoples in the name of democracy — was undermined by the messy realities of occupation. For many in the Middle East, the U.S. moved from broker to occupier, from helper to architect of rupture.

Abu Ghraib and the Damage to Moral Authority

If the structural damage of 2003 was political and administrative, some of the most damaging blows to the United States' standing were moral and symbolic. The Abu Ghraib scandal — photographs and reports of prisoner abuse by U.S. personnel at an Iraqi detention facility — became a global emblem of American hypocrisy. The Taguba investigation documented systemic failures and abuses, and the images that circulated worldwide did not just scandalize; they provided propaganda to extremist recruiters and deepened resentment among ordinary Iraqis who had hoped that liberation would bring dignity. <u>www.thetorturedatabase.org</u>

Abu Ghraib shows that the legitimacy of any external actor in a conflict hinges not merely on strategic goals but on behavior that conforms to international norms. When an intervener is seen to violate basic standards of treatment, it loses the moral platform necessary to mediate or rebuild. In bridge terms: you may have the heavy cranes to reconstruct a damaged span, but if the people on the far side do not trust you, your cranes accomplish little.

The Post-9/11 Moment: Counterterror, Drones, and Endless Presence

After the attacks of 11 September 2001, U.S. policy in the Middle East took on a new urgency and a different logic. The "Global War on Terror" prioritized preemption, targeted strikes, and counterinsurgency. The U.S. built vast detention infrastructures, carried out drone campaigns in Yemen and elsewhere, and invested heavily in special operations. For many governments, especially those aligned with Washington, counterterror cooperation became the currency of political favor. For many populations, however, the result was a constant perception of occupation and surveillance.

This era deepened a paradox: targeted strikes could eliminate dangerous leaders, but they often inflicted civilian casualties, displaced families, and left political grievances unresolved. The stability that durable peace requires cannot be purchased by strikes alone. In the absence of effective political solutions, the human geography of grievance — the very social fabric that bridges communities — continued to fray.

Libya, Syria, and the Limits of Selective Intervention

The Arab Spring tested U.S. policy again. In 2011, the U.S. and NATO intervened in Libya, ostensibly to prevent mass killings in Benghazi. That intervention succeeded in its narrow objective — it helped prevent a swift massacre — but it did not reckon with the aftermath: regime collapse, proliferation of weapons, and years of factional fighting. Libya's institutions had been personalist and brittle; without a credible plan for post-conflict governance, a liberated state became a failed state.

Syria posed the tougher dilemma. The Obama administration's public "red line" on chemical weapons was a moment of high stakes diplomacy and fraught messaging. While the U.S. eventually supported opposition elements and carried out limited strikes in response to chemical attacks, it did not deploy large-scale ground forces. Russia's later intervention turned the tide decisively in favor of Assad; the Syrian conflict therefore stands as a grim example of how local wars can become theatres for global competition, and how inconsistent external policy can leave civilians to bear the brunt.

Alliances and Arms: The Patron-Client Networks

Beyond overt interventions, America's role has long included arms transfers, training, and security guarantees to allies. Israel, above all, occupies a unique place in this matrix: a close military partner, principal recipient of U.S. foreign assistance, and political ally whose security Washington repeatedly affirms through Congressional appropriations and diplomatic backing. That relationship has solidified strategic ties but has also fed perceptions — particularly among Palestinians and Arab publics — that U.S. policy is not a neutral broker but a partisan supporter, complicating Washington's ability to mediate credibly. (See Congressional Research Service for detailed aid figures.) **FAS Project on Government SecrecyCongress**

Meanwhile, other partnerships — with Gulf monarchies, Turkey (until recent strains), Jordan, and Egypt — have helped preserve American influence. But these relationships sometimes propped up autocratic governance and security-first agendas at the expense of political liberalization. In bridge terms: the U.S. often maintained sturdy guardrails for regimes it preferred while leaving the pedestrian crosswalks of civic life unpaved.

The Unintended Consequences: Vacuums, Extremists, and Refugees

A recurring pattern emerges when interventions lack credible exit strategies or fail to rebuild governance: **vacuum → fragmentation → extremism**. The 2003 Iraq war's institutional dismantling produced precisely that sequence, as did the weak post-liberation settlement in Libya. One of the most visible results was the rise of ISIS: a group that capitalized on Sunni grievances, state failure, and regional instability to seize territory in 2013–2014 and declare a caliphate that lasted until a sustained international and local campaign rolled it back. The speed with which ISIS gathered power — including the fall of Mosul in 2014 — was a stark demonstration of how quickly a collapsed political order can produce a new, transnational threat. **Wilson CenterUnited States**

Institute of Peace

Refugee flows are another consequence. Wars precipitated or amplified by external intervention produce diasporas that remake politics across borders. Camps become long-term ecosystems where trauma is inherited and where diasporic networks carry claims and funding across continents. The human geography of displacement — the permanent archipelago of camps and slums — is partly the product of broken bridges that foreign policy promised to repair but left to drift.

The Credibility Problem: Why the United States Struggles to Be Seen as a Neutral Builder

If the U.S. is to play a constructive role in the Middle East, it must be perceived as credible. That perception is shaped by several factors:

Consistency. Policy swings from interventionism to restraint make the U.S. look unpredictable. Credible bridge-building requires patient, steady engagement.

Impartiality. Being seen as disproportionately aligned to one party undercuts mediation. Close ties with Israel, while strategic, complicate the U.S. role as an honest broker in Palestinian-Israeli negotiations.

Legitimacy of means. Actions like Abu Ghraib or indefinite detention undermine the moral authority necessary to persuade parties to compromise.

Exit strategies and institution-building. Interventions without plans for governance and reconstruction create more harm than good.

These are not abstract failures but practical constraints on policy design. They explain why the U.S. has, at times, been better at building partial bridges (e.g., Camp David) and worse at sustaining whole crossings.

Toward a More Constructive American Role: Lessons and Design Principles

If the U.S. is to shift from a pattern of intermittent repairs and destructive interventions to a role that genuinely rebuilds, a reorientation along several lines is necessary:

Prioritize political solutions over kinetic fixes. Military force should be a last resort; diplomacy, penalized by impatience, must be given time and resources. Camp David succeeded because Washington concentrated attention and patience.

Plan the exit from the start. Interventions must be coupled with realistic plans for governance, security-sector reform, and civilian institutions. Occupation without such a plan produces vacuums.

Center local ownership. External actors can provide resources and guarantees but must not substitute for local legitimacy. Reconstruction that appears imposed will not last.

Use multilateral frameworks. Where possible, the U.S. should work through coalitions and with international institutions to share costs, increase legitimacy, and reduce perceptions of unilateralism.

Match security assistance with governance conditionalities. Aid and arms should incentivize accountability, not merely suppress dissent.

Address root causes. Economic development, rule of law, and inclusion are long-term investments that prevent the recruitment of young people into armed groups.

These principles are not doctrinaire prescriptions; they are design heuristics that recognize the ethics and engineering of bridge repair require both tools and trust.

A Story of Two Bridges: A Composite Vignette

To make the stakes concrete, consider a composite narrative.

In 2002, Omar, a schoolteacher in a mid-sized Iraqi town, worries about his students. The authoritarian regime's security services watch the curriculum; his friends' sons are conscripted; the region is tense. In 2003, coalition forces arrive; Omar hears that liberation will bring schools that teach civic values. But months later, the municipal offices lie empty, the hospitals don't have medicine, and the orphaned boys find work with militias that promise wages and security. Omar's town becomes a place of checkpoints and competing powers. Ten years later, one of those boys travels to Syria and returns radicalized. Omar's grandchildren grow up in a world where the bridge to normalcy was cut midway.

Contrast that with a different composite: In 1979, a farmer in the Sinai whose family had sold olive oil for generations sees diplomats arrive in Cairo; months later, a peace treaty reduces the chance of cross-border raids. Trade resumes; a market opens. For a while, the bridge holds.

Those two simple stories — one of a broken repair, one of a partial success — illustrate one truth of this chapter: American policy can create durable crossings, but only when diplomacy, long-term institution building, and local legitimacy are prioritized over short-term tactical gains.

Conclusion: America's Responsibility — Not Just Capacity

Power matters in the Middle East. The United States possesses unparalleled military capability and diplomatic weight. That combination means Washington can shape whether the region's bridge is repaired or left to drift. But with capacity comes responsibility. The pattern of U.S. policy — alternating between bridge-building diplomacy and heavy-handed intervention — has contributed to cycles of instability. If the central aim of this book is to explain why the Middle East's conflicts continue, then one of the clearest answers is that major external actors, most prominently the United States, have too often treated the bridge as something to be used for strategic crossings rather than something to be preserved for all.

Repairing the bridge will demand different American judgments: humility in the face of complex local politics, patience to support institutions rather than personalities, and a willingness to bind action to international law and multilateral oversight. Above all, it will require asking a difficult question: are immediate tactical goals worth the long-term health of the crossing? If the answer is no, then the United States must reorder its priorities.

In the chapters that follow we will examine how other international actors — Russia, China, and the United Nations — have either helped or hindered the repair. We will also move from diagnosis to design: taking the lessons of past U.S. policy as a cautionary manual for what bridge-building must avoid, and what it must embrace. The bridge is not beyond repair; but it will not be stitched back together by power alone. It will be mended by a strategy that prizes institutions, justice, and the slow work of trust.

Key sources for this chapter's anchor facts:

Camp David Accords and U.S. role. <u>Office of the Historian</u>

Oslo Accords and the U.S. sponsorship. <u>Office of the Historian</u>

Iraq Survey Group (Duelfer) findings on WMD claims and post-war assessments. <u>GovInfo</u>

Taguba inquiry into detainee abuses at Abu Ghraib. <u>www. thetorturedatabase.org</u>

Timelines and analyses of ISIS's rapid expansion in 2013–2014, including Mosul's fall. <u>Wilson CenterUnited States Institute of Peace</u>

It is impossible to tell the story of the Middle East's broken bridge without reckoning with the United States. For more than seven decades, Washington has played a role at nearly every fracture and every attempted repair. Sometimes the U.S. has appeared as an architect, hammer in hand, trying to rebuild. At other times, it has been the wrecking ball, knocking away supports in pursuit of strategic advantage.

Washington Enters the Region

At the close of World War II, as Europe's empires crumbled, the U.S. emerged as the new external power in the Middle East. Oil was the lifeblood of industrial economies, and Saudi Arabia, newly allied with Washington, held vast reserves. Containment of communism soon followed as the second pillar of U.S. engagement. The Truman Doctrine of 1947 made the Middle East a frontline in the Cold War, and American policymakers quickly realized the region's geography — the Suez Canal, the Persian Gulf, the Levant — was too vital to ignore.

The Peace Broker's Image

In 1978, America presented itself as a master builder of bridges. President Jimmy Carter hosted Anwar Sadat of Egypt and Menachem Begin of Israel at Camp David, mediating the accords that ended three decades of war. The bridge built at Camp David was not perfect — it left Palestinians still stranded — but it showed that U.S. diplomacy could change the course of history.

The 1990s brought another attempt at bridge-building with the Oslo Accords. In the famous image from the White House lawn, President Bill Clinton stood between Yitzhak Rabin and Yasser Arafat, arms outstretched, guiding their handshake. For a brief moment, the world believed that America might guide Israelis and Palestinians across the chasm to peace. Yet the bridge collapsed once more, undone by mistrust, violence, and the steady expansion of settlements.

The Interventionist's Hammer

The U.S. has not always built — often, it has broken. The 1991 Gulf War, launched to expel Saddam Hussein from Kuwait, left Iraq battered but intact. Twelve years later, in 2003, America returned not as liberator but as occupier. The invasion of Iraq toppled Saddam but shattered the Iraqi state. Ministries were looted, the army disbanded, sectarian militias rose, and civil war erupted. Out of this chaos came the Islamic State, a movement that fed on the ruins left behind.

For millions in the region, America ceased to be seen as a broker of peace and became instead the symbol of intervention, drone strikes, and indefinite military presence. The U.S. spoke of freedom but was remembered for Abu Ghraib. It promised democracy but was associated with instability.

In Iran, the bridge of sovereignty was weakened long before the modern Middle East was carved by mandates and foreign rulers. Though never colonized outright like its neighbors, Iran was bound by invisible chains of influence. Britain and Russia divided it into spheres of control in 1907, treating the nation less as a sovereign state and more as a buffer zone in their imperial chessboard. The Persian people watched as their land remained whole on the map but fractured in authority. The bridge of independence stood, but its foundations were not their own.

Oil became both blessing and curse. The Anglo-Persian Oil Company turned Iran's natural wealth into a colonial asset, enriching foreign powers while leaving Iranians with little to show. The bridge of prosperity was promised, but it was built for others to cross. During both world wars, Iran was occupied—its railways, fields, and cities serving the strategies of others. Even when the Shah sat on his throne, the true weight of power often rested in distant capitals.

The moment the people tried to rebuild the bridge themselves, it was broken again. In 1951, Prime Minister Mohammad Mossadegh sought to nationalize Iran's oil and place its riches back in Iranian hands. For a brief moment, the beams of sovereignty looked as if they could finally hold. But in 1953, a coup orchestrated by Britain and the United States toppled him, pulling apart the structure before it could bear weight. What remained was not a bridge of independence, but one of dependency, patched together by foreign intervention.

This is where Iran's story links with the wider pattern of modern U.S. involvement in the region. Just as Iraq's fragile bridge was dismantled in 2003, Iran's was shaken decades earlier by the same foreign hand. Both nations became case studies in how intervention, even when framed as protection or progress, often left societies fractured and mistrustful. The broken bridges of Iraq and Iran are not separate ruins but adjoining spans on the same road, each weakened by the weight of external designs.

The legacy runs deep. Iran's revolutions, its distrust of the West, and its fierce insistence on self-determination are born from bridges broken too many times by hands that were not Iranian. Iraq's descent into chaos after Saddam, too, reflects the price of dismantling a state without building a true replacement. Together, their stories remind us that the colonial legacies of Sykes–Picot and the mandates did not end with Europe's retreat—they continued in new forms of power, new forms of control.

Like Iraq, Syria, Yemen, Gaza, and Israel, Iran's bridge is part of the larger story of the Middle East—a story of crossings built and broken, of peoples striving for passage across chasms of history, power, and memory. And until those bridges can be rebuilt not by outsiders but by the people themselves, the crossings will remain unstable, haunted by the weight of what has already fallen.

The Broken Bridge and America

For the Middle East, America has always been a paradox. To some, it arrives as the engineer of peace, unrolling blueprints for bridges of diplomacy. To others, it is the demolition crew, setting charges beneath fragile structures that had barely begun to stand. America builds bridges that shine under the flashbulbs of history, but often abandons them halfway, leaving travelers stranded between shores. And when it destroys, the wreckage is measured not in years but in generations.

Builders of Hope: When Bridges Held

There are moments when the United States has reached across the divides of the Middle East and laid down beams of connection strong enough to hold. One of the most enduring examples remains the **Camp David Accords of 1978.**

The world remembers the images: Egyptian President Anwar Sadat, Israeli Prime Minister Menachem Begin, and U.S. President Jimmy Carter clasping hands. Behind the picture was thirteen days of grueling negotiation, where mistrust weighed heavily, and every word felt like a plank precariously laid over a chasm. Yet, out of the strain came a treaty that ended decades of open war between Israel and Egypt. For the first time, an Arab nation formally recognized Israel, and Egypt regained the Sinai Peninsula.

This was America as bridge-builder: patient, persistent, and committed to carrying two enemies across a divide that had seemed impossible to traverse. The bridge still stands today. Strained? Yes. Contested? Certainly. But it has endured conflict, uprisings, and shifting alliances. It has proven that some structures, if carefully built, can weather the storms of history.

A similar moment came in the **1990s with the Oslo Accords.** President Bill Clinton presided over another iconic handshake—this time between Israeli Prime Minister Yitzhak Rabin and Palestinian leader Yasser Arafat. For a brief moment, the world held its breath, believing that perhaps the longest-standing chasm in the Middle East might finally be bridged.

But Oslo's structure was never completed. Its beams were thin, its foundations unsettled. Rabin's assassination, waves of suicide bombings, and the unyielding growth of Israeli settlements shook the bridge until it cracked. By the early 2000s, Oslo had become a skeleton of promise:

a scaffold of what could have been, suspended in air, unable to carry its people across.

Breakers of Trust: When Bridges Collapsed

If Camp David was America the builder, then **Iraq in 2003** was America the breaker.

The U.S.-led invasion toppled Saddam Hussein, but in tearing down the regime, it also dismantled the very framework of the Iraqi state. Ministries were looted, the army dissolved, and the fragile bridge of national sovereignty was blasted apart. In the rubble, sectarian militias fought for dominance, and from the fractures rose the Islamic State, a movement born from the void left behind.

What had been promised as liberation came to be remembered as occupation. For Iraqis, America's bridge was not one of freedom but of ruin—a crossing destroyed before it could even serve its purpose.

This was not the first time Washington's presence left ruins. In **Lebanon, 1982**, American Marines arrived as peacekeepers during civil war. Yet after the devastating suicide bombing that killed 241 servicemen, the U.S. withdrew abruptly. To many Lebanese, it seemed that America's bridges were temporary—built when convenient, abandoned when costly.

The pattern repeated elsewhere. In **Afghanistan**, America's twenty-year war ended with the Taliban's return, the bridge of stability collapsing as U.S. forces departed. In **Libya**, airstrikes helped topple Gaddafi, but no stable state replaced him. The crossing to democracy crumbled into chaos. And in **Syria**, Washington's half-steps—supporting some rebels while striking others—added complexity to an already shattered landscape.

Each of these stories became part of the region's memory: bridges half-built, bridges destroyed, bridges that led nowhere.

Bridges of Power: Allies, Arms, and Resentment

Not all of America's bridges were built for peace. Some were built for power.

With Israel, the connection has been reinforced with billions of dollars in military aid, forming a steel bridge that remains unshakable. Egypt, rewarded for its peace with Israel, became another permanent ally. The Gulf monarchies—Saudi Arabia, Qatar, the UAE—stand on bridges made of oil, energy markets, and arms sales.

But these are bridges of inequality. They carry weapons and wealth, but rarely justice. To ordinary citizens of the region, these alliances often looked like narrow crossings designed for the powerful, leaving everyone else in the dust.

Drone strikes in Yemen and Pakistan, sanctions that punished civilians more than regimes, and the infamous images from **Abu Ghraib prison** etched into memory—these moments reinforced the belief that America's bridges were never meant for everyone. They were structures of control, built to favor some while bypassing others.

The Broken Bridge of Iran

Perhaps no story illustrates America's paradox more than its relationship with Iran.

In **1953**, the U.S. helped orchestrate a coup against Prime Minister Mohammad Mossadegh, punishing him for daring to nationalize oil. The fragile bridge of democracy was broken before it could fully stand. For decades after, Washington propped up the Shah, whose reign collapsed in the 1979 Revolution. From then on, America became Iran's great adversary.

Every attempt at diplomacy—from nuclear negotiations to prisoner swaps—has felt like laying planks on a bridge already riddled with cracks. Each step forward seems to break beneath the weight of mistrust. For over seventy years, Iran and America have stared at one another across a broken bridge, unwilling—or unable—to rebuild.

If the history of American involvement in the Middle East is a story of broken bridges, then the future must be a story of rebuilding. For more than a century, treaties, invasions, revolutions, and alliances have determined whether the bridges connecting the region stand or collapse. But concrete and steel are not enough. At the heart of every structure lies something more fragile and more enduring: the choices of people. Leaders, youth, and the next generation will decide whether the broken bridge of the Middle East remains a ruin or becomes a crossing that carries entire societies toward peace.

History remembers the rare moments when leaders have laid bold beams across the divide. Anwar Sadat, boarding a plane to Jerusalem in 1977, took a step that no Arab leader had dared before. Yitzhak Rabin, once a hardened general, stood on the White House lawn in 1993 and clasped Yasser Arafat's hand. King Hussein of Jordan, often quiet in demeanor, negotiated tirelessly to steady his nation between neighbors at war. These were not acts of weakness but of courage—the decisions of leaders who believed that even after decades of bloodshed, bridges could still be built.

Their legacies echo into the present. In 2020, the **Abraham Accords** opened another fragile crossing. Israel and the United Arab Emirates signed a normalization agreement, soon joined by Bahrain, Morocco, and Sudan. Flights began linking Tel Aviv with Abu Dhabi and Manama. Business delegations formed joint ventures in technology and tourism. Israeli families visited Dubai's markets; Emirati students toured Jerusalem's old streets. For the first time in decades, a new kind of bridge was being tested—not one built on temporary ceasefires, but on shared economic interests and cultural exchanges.

The accords were controversial. Some Palestinians felt betrayed, arguing that bridges built without them were incomplete. And indeed, no crossing in the region can last if it excludes the people most affected by its arches. Yet, the accords remain an undeniable example of what political will can achieve when leaders choose dialogue over deadlock. They remind us that history bends not only under the weight of armies, but also under the pens of leaders daring enough to sign their names to new futures.

Still, treaties alone are not enough. Bridges must be reinforced with real foundations: solutions to refugee crises, opportunities for youth employment, and healing for the wounds of war. Without these, even the most daring political spans risk collapse.

If leaders provide the scaffolding, youth provide the labor, creativity, and spirit to bring new bridges to life. Across the Middle East, young people inherit fractured crossings: checkpoints, refugee camps, drone-shadowed skies, and memories of war passed down like family heirlooms. Yet they also inherit something else—imagination.

One powerful example is **Seeds of Peace**, a program that brings together teenagers from Israel, Palestine, Jordan, Egypt, and beyond. In summer camps in Maine and ongoing initiatives across the region, these young people—who grew up seeing one another as soldiers, threats, or occupiers—sit side by side in classrooms and dining halls. They share stories of loss, of fear, of aspiration. They argue, they cry, they laugh, they play soccer together. By the time they return home, they carry something rare: the knowledge that the "enemy" has a human face. In the metaphor of the bridge, they are laying planks of empathy across a chasm carved by history.

In **Gaza**, despite blockade and hardship, youth-led NGOs like *Gaza Sky Geeks* provide training in coding, entrepreneurship, and digital literacy. Here, innovation itself becomes a form of resistance—not to peace, but to despair. Every app coded, every startup launched, is a stone placed in a bridge leading outward, connecting Gaza's youth to a global economy that had once seemed forever out of reach.

In **Iraq**, young innovators in Baghdad and Erbil are transforming the rubble of war into hubs of creativity. Startups in renewable energy, agriculture, and digital services now employ both Sunni and Shia, Arab and Kurd. These ventures, though modest, are bridges in their own right: practical crossings that prove coexistence is not a utopian dream but a daily possibility.

And in **Iran**, where sanctions have restricted opportunities, young filmmakers, coders, and artists share their work online, bypassing isolation to connect with audiences around the globe. A short film screened at a European festival, a mobile app downloaded abroad, a digital art piece sold as an NFT—each act is a bridge, slender but real, stretching across political divides toward a shared human story.

Youth movements are not free of struggle. Many of these initiatives face harassment, surveillance, or suppression. Yet the persistence of young builders demonstrates a simple truth: where leaders hesitate, youth often leap.

The children of today—whether in Aleppo, Gaza, Mosul, or Tehran—will inherit whatever bridges their elders build. They will either cross structures sturdy enough to bear commerce, culture, and community, or they will wander among ruins, learning once again how to survive without passage.

Education is the cornerstone of this inheritance. **UNRWA schools for Palestinian refugees**—crowded, underfunded, yet vital—provide a bridge to literacy and hope for millions. In Yemen, community-driven programs distribute books where food aid struggles to reach, reminding families that the mind must also be nourished. In Jordan, Syrian refugee children attend special double-shift schools where local students study in the morning and displaced students in the afternoon. Each classroom, however modest, is a bridge: a fragile but vital crossing into the future.

And beyond formal education, there are subtler bridges—storytelling, cultural memory, family traditions—that carry children across the chasm of conflict. A grandmother in a Palestinian camp telling stories of orchards she once tended; a Syrian father teaching his children to read in the dust of a refugee camp; a young Yemeni artist painting murals over bomb-scarred walls—these are planks of identity, connection, and resilience.

America cannot build these bridges alone, but it can supply the materials. Scholarships, cultural exchange programs, reconstruction aid, and support for youth-led initiatives can strengthen local builders. Diplomatic patience can replace military haste. Consistency, rather than abrupt intervention or withdrawal, can help reinforce what leaders and youth already begin.

The paradox of America need not remain eternal. The question is whether Washington will continue a pattern of half-built bridges and sudden demolitions—or whether it will commit to steady, quiet construction, letting those who must walk the bridges take the lead in deciding where they are built.

The broken bridge is not destiny. Across the Middle East, leaders can choose to extend hands beyond division. Youth can imagine new crossings where their elders saw only barriers. The next generation deserves to inherit not ruins but pathways. And America, for all its contradictions, holds influence to reinforce or weaken these efforts.

Bridges in the Middle East have collapsed under empire, mandate, revolution, and occupation. Yet bridges, by their very nature, are meant to be rebuilt. The test of our time—of leaders, of youth, of the next generation, and of America itself—is whether they will summon the will and wisdom to lay stones where ruins lie, to span the divide not halfway but fully, and to build crossings strong enough to endure the weight of history and the hope of tomorrow.

Russia's Influence — The Return of the Bear

While the world's eyes often focused on Washington, Russia — first under the banner of the Soviet Union and later under Vladimir Putin — quietly but deliberately carved a presence in the Middle East. Where America frequently preached democracy, freedom, and ideals that sometimes never reached the ground, Moscow offered something more immediate: protection, weapons, and the blunt force of geopolitical power. In a region historically riddled with betrayal, occupation, and colonial legacies, this offer carried undeniable appeal. But like all bridges built on power rather than trust, Russia's path left much of the population stranded while elevating leaders who owed allegiance, not accountability, to their people.

The Soviet Era: Architect of Regimes

In the mid-20th century, the Cold War reshaped the Middle East. The United States, allied with Israel and regional monarchies, promoted a vision of order that often sidelined local aspirations. Across the region, Arab leaders wary of Western influence looked eastward, toward Moscow, whose ideology and military might offered an alternative.

For the Soviet Union, the Middle East was both an ideological and strategic playground. It was a theater where anti-colonialism, nationalism, and socialist ambition intersected. Egypt under Gamal Abdel Nasser became the jewel in Moscow's crown. Soviet engineers and technicians constructed the Aswan High Dam, a colossal infrastructure project that controlled the Nile's flow and symbolized modernity. Soviet advisors trained pilots and military officers, embedding Moscow's influence within Egypt's defense apparatus. For many Egyptians, the Soviets were saviors, builders, and teachers. Yet for others, they were outsiders imposing a foreign model that sometimes ignored the nuanced realities of life along the Nile.

In Syria and Iraq, Soviet influence took a more militarized form. Tanks, fighter jets, and missiles flowed across borders, equipping regimes that felt threatened by both internal dissent and external pressure. For Hafez al-Assad in Syria, the USSR offered survival in a volatile neighborhood; for Saddam Hussein, Soviet arms provided the backbone for regional ambition. Across these alliances, Moscow's strategy was clear: support regimes that would support Moscow, regardless of their popularity at home.

But these bridges were double-edged. They fortified governments, but they often left the people's grievances unaddressed. Ordinary citizens, caught between ambition and repression, rarely benefited from Moscow's largesse. The USSR's bridges were engineered for rulers, not for the societies they governed.

Retreat: The Fall of the Soviet Bridge

The collapse of the Soviet Union in 1991 was seismic. For decades, Moscow had been a constant, a looming presence in the Middle East. Suddenly, that presence evaporated. Russia's military contracts faltered, diplomatic attention waned, and alliances weakened. Leaders who had depended on Soviet support were forced to adapt to a new world order, often turning to the United States or regional powers for survival.

For a decade, it seemed the bear had left the Middle East entirely. The bridges constructed over decades lay in ruins, symbolic rather than functional. Yet, even in retreat, Moscow's shadow lingered. Memories of Soviet support remained, particularly among leaders who had tasted both the power and the protection it offered. These memories would prove vital when Russia returned, not as an ideologue, but as a pragmatic power broker.

The Syrian Gamble: The Bear Returns

By 2015, the Middle East had become a landscape of desperation. Syria, once a relatively stable state, was fractured by civil war, sectarian divides, and the rise of extremist factions. Bashar al-Assad's regime teetered on the edge of collapse. Rebel forces advanced toward Damascus, and extremist groups like ISIS captured territory with alarming speed. The international community watched in alarm, yet few were willing to intervene decisively.

Into this chaos stepped Russia. With precision and resolve, Moscow intervened militarily, strategically, and diplomatically. Russian fighter jets began airstrikes against rebel-held areas, often using advanced targeting technology to strike decisively, yet frequently causing civilian casualties. On the diplomatic front, Russian representatives wielded veto power in the United Nations, shielding Damascus from sanctions and international censure.

Moscow's intervention reshaped the war. Assad's forces regained momentum; territories that seemed lost were retaken. The message was unmistakable: Russia was back, capable of exerting power far beyond its borders, and willing to defend the regimes that aligned with it.

Yet this return was transactional. Military bases were expanded, weapons contracts signed, and arms demonstrations staged for potential buyers. Syria was no charity case; it was a proving ground for Russia's renewed regional ambitions. In the process, Moscow rebuilt its bridge to the Middle East — not through reconciliation or democratic principles, but through the projection of force and strategic indispensability.

Energy, Arms, and the Architecture of Influence

Russia's influence stretches beyond Syria. Energy and arms have become the twin pillars of its Middle Eastern strategy. By cooperating with Saudi Arabia in OPEC+, Russia wields influence over global oil prices, affecting economies from Tokyo to Cairo. Russian weapons systems are sold to Algeria, Egypt, and Gulf states, each deal reinforcing Moscow's role as an indispensable power broker.

These transactions are more than commerce; they are bridges of influence, each brick laid to bind leaders to Moscow's orbit. Loyalty is rewarded with protection, rebellion punished with ruin. For strongmen, Russia's approach is appealing — a reliable backer against both internal revolt and external threats. For ordinary citizens, it is suffocating: their fate becomes secondary to the survival of regimes, the stability of alliances, and the calculation of global powers.

The Broken Bridge and Russia

The contrast with the United States is stark. American interventions often promise freedom but leave destruction in their wake, breaking bridges between communities, governments, and international partners. Russia's model is subtler yet no less consequential. Its bridges are built not to connect societies but to consolidate power for those at the top.

In the Middle East, this has profound implications. Where Washington sometimes undermines governance through idealistic overreach, Moscow fortifies authoritarian structures. Its promise is simple: obey, survive, and thrive; resist, and face obliteration. The bear's bridges may last, but they span rulers rather than people, power rather than progress. For populations caught beneath, the river remains uncrossed.

Russia's influence is thus a study in contrasts. It is a bridge built with purpose, discipline, and permanence, yet invisible to the majority it purports to protect. It is a lesson in how power can stabilize regimes while leaving societies stranded, and how in the Middle East, the broken bridges of history are often repaired only for the benefit of the few, not the many.

China's Strategic Interests: The Silent Builder

In the Middle East, where history has been written in blood, oil, and the ambitions of external powers, China presents a distinct approach. Unlike the hammer of Washington, often crashing through states in the name of democracy, or the shield of Moscow, which propped up regimes in exchange for loyalty, Beijing acts as a quiet builder. It does not promise liberation, nor does it intervene militarily. Instead, it lays down roads, ports, and fiber optic cables, stitching together a fractured region with infrastructure and trade agreements. China's presence is subtle, transactional, and carefully calculated: bridges of commerce in a region riddled with broken social and political ones.

Yet these bridges, though impressive, carry only certain burdens and benefits. They often serve governments and elites, leaving ordinary citizens, refugees, and displaced communities watching silently from the banks. In this chapter, we trace China's footprint across Iran, Iraq, Egypt, and the Gulf, exploring both the tangible achievements of the

Belt and Road Initiative and the human consequences of this quiet form of influence.

Oil and Trade: Lifelines of Influence

China's reliance on Middle Eastern oil has long defined its regional strategy. As the world's largest importer of crude, China depends on the Gulf for energy security. Saudi Arabia, Iraq, and Iran form a lifeline: pipelines and ports funnel millions of barrels to feed the engines of China's industrial growth.

In Baghdad, Omar, an oil engineer with Iraq's state-run pipeline authority, remembers the arrival of Chinese teams in the 2010s. *"They did not speak of politics or ideology,"* he said. *"They asked about efficiency, schedules, safety. When the work was done, the oil flowed. That was enough for them. That was enough for us too — as long as we were paid."*

The pragmatism of Beijing's approach allows it to navigate a region of competing interests. Unlike the United States, often drawn into disputes over Israel, Syria, or regional sectarianism, China focuses on commerce. Unlike Russia, which intervenes to preserve authoritarian regimes, Beijing prioritizes stability sufficient to guarantee its energy supply. This strategy of restraint has often allowed China to maintain cordial relations across rival factions, quietly threading its influence where others collide.

In southern Iran, near the port city of Bandar Abbas, Iranian dockworker Leila describes the arrival of Chinese engineers to expand port facilities. *"They built quickly, almost like a storm passing through,"* she recalls. *"The cranes arrived, the warehouses rose, and suddenly, we were handling shipments we had never seen before. But the people who live here, who rely on fishing or local markets, saw little of it. The port belonged to the ships, the oil, and the contracts. Not to us."*

China's strategy is unmistakable: secure energy and trade flows, invest in infrastructure to protect these lifelines, and remain largely neutral in the politics that could disrupt them. Its influence is pragmatic, deliberate, and profitable — but often invisible to the populations living under its projects.

The Belt and Road Initiative: Concrete Bridges Across Contested Lands

In 2013, China announced the Belt and Road Initiative (BRI), a sprawling strategy to connect Asia, Africa, and Europe through trade, infrastructure, and investment. For the Middle East, it promised billions in projects: ports, highways, railways, and industrial zones stretching across deserts, coasts, and river valleys.

In Egypt, the city of Ain Sokhna has been transformed by Chinese investment. The port, once a minor logistics hub on the Red Sea, now handles massive container traffic linking Egypt to China and beyond. Hassan, a dockworker, describes the first cranes arriving: *"They worked day and night. We saw offices, warehouses, even dormitories for the workers. Everything was new. But I realized we were building something for trade, not for ourselves. It was our labor, their bridge."*

These projects are concrete, tangible, and highly visible — impressive bridges over geography, commerce, and time. Yet they often bypass local communities in terms of social benefit. Schools, hospitals, and public services rarely accompany highways or industrial zones. In Baghdad's industrial suburbs, Iraqi small business owner Mustafa reflects on Chinese involvement in local industrial zones: *"They bring machines, they bring jobs, yes. But most of the skilled positions go to Chinese engineers or to people with connections. We have roads, but no real opportunities. The bridge looks impressive, but it doesn't carry us."*

In Iran, the railways connecting Tehran to the Persian Gulf have facilitated trade and commerce, but they have also introduced new tensions. Farmers in central Iran complain that Chinese-run logistics companies import products that undercut local markets, forcing them to compete against goods shipped from abroad. Amir, a wheat farmer, says, *"We have roads now, yes. But we cannot sell our crops without competing with imports. The bridge carries commerce, but it leaves us behind."*

In Oman, China has invested in the port of Duqm, transforming it into a strategic node for international shipping. Fatima, a local teacher, describes how the project changed her community: *"They brought roads, electricity, and even schools for the workers' children. But our children, who live here, still walk miles to old, overcrowded schools. The port is magnificent, but the benefits are divided. We watch, but we cannot cross."*

Diplomatic Neutrality: The Power of Silence

China's influence is not only material; it is diplomatic. Beijing emphasizes non-interference, carefully balancing relations across rival states. It maintains ties with Israel and Palestine, Saudi Arabia and Iran, often stepping into diplomatic gaps left by Washington and Moscow.

In 2023, China orchestrated a surprising breakthrough: a symbolic thaw between Riyadh and Tehran. Delegates met in Beijing, shook hands under the Chinese flag, and issued statements of intent for reconciliation. Analysts hailed the event as a triumph of silent diplomacy: China could broker agreements where traditional powers failed.

Yet for citizens caught in decades-long conflicts, these gestures often feel abstract. Refugees in Syrian camps along the Iraqi border do not see railways or ports as solutions to their daily struggles. In Amman, Syrian teacher Rania remarks: *"The highways, the ports, the cranes — they are grand. But what about schools for our children, hospitals for our sick, or jobs for the unemployed? China builds, yes. But it does not repair hearts."*

China's diplomatic model complements its economic one: it builds bridges of influence that are visible to governments, companies, and global markets, but often silent to those most in need.

Human Stories from the Ground

Across the Middle East, the Belt and Road Initiative has altered lives in ways both visible and invisible.

In southern Iraq, the port of Umm Qasr has expanded under Chinese investment. Longtime dockworker Saeed describes the changes: *"The cranes are huge, the ships are bigger. But our pay hasn't changed much. The port belongs to the contracts, the cargo, the companies. Not to us."*

In Cairo's industrial zones, small textile owners complain that Chinese machinery and production lines outcompete their family businesses. Fatima, who runs a local workshop, sighs: *"We see new roads, new factories. But they are for exports, not for local growth. We are building the bridge, but we cannot walk on it."*

In Tehran, farmers near the rail lines notice that imported goods arrive faster and cheaper than what they produce. Amir says, *"We have connections now, yes. But our livelihood is at risk. The bridge carries trade, but not fairness."*

In Oman, youth in Duqm watch the Chinese-built port thrive while local opportunities remain limited. Fatima, a teacher, observes: *"We have infrastructure, yes. But our community feels like spectators. The bridge carries commerce, not our dreams."*

These stories reveal a central truth: China's bridges, though material and impressive, often bypass the social fractures that define the Middle East. They connect continents but rarely reconcile communities. They facilitate trade but not justice. They bring steel and concrete but not hope to refugees, farmers, and workers who live along the riverbanks of broken promises.

The Broken Bridge and China

In the calculus of the Middle East, China represents a new kind of power. Its influence is quiet, deliberate, and profitable. It builds roads, ports, railways, and industrial zones — tangible symbols of connection and progress. Its diplomacy is measured, balanced, and non-interventionist.

Yet these bridges are limited in moral and social scope. They enrich governments and elites, but rarely transform the daily realities of citizens caught in cycles of war, displacement, and economic vulnerability. Highways may stretch across deserts, and cranes may rise above ports, but the fractures of justice, reconciliation, and human security remain unaddressed.

For those living on the ground — workers, teachers, farmers, and refugees — China's bridges are impressive to behold, but largely inaccessible. They carry commerce and opportunity for some, but leave millions stranded, watching from the banks as the river of suffering flows beneath.

In a region scarred by broken promises, foreign interventions, and shattered social structures, China builds silently, efficiently, and strategically. Its bridges are real, durable, and monumental — yet incomplete. They connect trade, not trust; steel, not justice; roads, not reconciliation.

And in the Middle East, where every bridge has been contested, destroyed, or corrupted, China's silent construction serves as a reminder: infrastructure can span continents, but without moral and social vision, it cannot heal the broken bridges of human society.

The United Nations and International Law: Bridges of Paper and Principle

In the Middle East, a land scarred by centuries of conquest, empire, and ideological struggle, the United Nations often stands as a symbol of hope—or at least of structure. Its resolutions, treaties, and peacekeeping missions promise order, legality, and protection for those caught in the crossfire of war, political upheaval, and foreign interventions. Yet the reality on the ground frequently exposes the limits of these promises. For civilians, refugees, and local communities, the UN's bridges are often invisible, fragile, or only partially constructed.

The UN was born from the ashes of World War II, a global attempt to prevent repetition of the kind of destruction that had engulfed Europe and Asia. Its charter enshrined principles of sovereignty, collective security, and human rights, intending to hold nations accountable to a shared moral and legal standard. In the Middle East, however, the UN's ideals have often collided with the complex realities of history, geography, and politics. The result is a recurring paradox: a bridge exists in principle, yet many cannot cross it.

The Charter and Early Resolutions: Paper Bridges

The foundation of the UN's engagement in the Middle East is rooted in its charter, which emphasizes sovereignty, the protection of human rights, and the maintenance of international peace. From the 1947 partition of Palestine to the Arab-Israeli conflicts of the mid-20th century, UN resolutions have attempted to mediate disputes, often under immense pressure from global and regional powers.

For instance, **UN Resolution 181**, which proposed the partition of Palestine into Jewish and Arab states, laid out a framework intended to provide peace and legitimacy. Yet the resolution immediately sparked conflict, as local communities resisted the imposition of boundaries decided in faraway chambers of diplomacy. Palestinians in Jerusalem, Nablus, and Gaza recall families uprooted, homes destroyed, and communities divided.

Later, **UN Resolution 242**, following the Six-Day War in 1967, demanded Israeli withdrawal from occupied territories and recognition of the sovereignty of all states in the region. On paper, it established a moral and legal guideline for peace. In practice, it became a battlefield of interpretation. Diplomatic language, debated in New York and Geneva, often seemed irrelevant to civilians enduring occupation, checkpoints, and daily insecurity.

Amal, a schoolteacher in Ramallah, remembers her father's words from the 1970s: *"They write resolutions in New York. They pass laws in Geneva. But when tanks roll down the street, no one checks the fine print. Paper does not stop bullets."*

This tension between international legal ideals and the reality of local suffering illustrates the central challenge of the UN in the Middle East: a bridge exists, but its span is often theoretical. The structure is present, yet many remain stranded on the banks of injustice.

Peacekeeping Missions: Soldiers Between Shadows

The UN began deploying peacekeeping missions in the Middle East as early as the late 1940s. These missions, composed of troops from neutral or non-aligned nations, were tasked with observing ceasefires, separating warring factions, and protecting civilians. Yet their effectiveness has been limited by lack of enforcement authority, political constraints, and local hostility.

In Lebanon, for example, the United Nations Interim Force in Lebanon (UNIFIL) was deployed to supervise Israeli withdrawals, maintain ceasefires, and support Lebanese sovereignty. UN soldiers patrolled roads scarred by landmines, mediated disputes between local militias and external forces, and occasionally protected civilians caught in crossfire.

Sergeant Amina, a peacekeeper from Kenya stationed in Tyre, recounts the challenges she faced: *"We could observe, report, and sometimes intervene. But when missiles struck villages, there was little we could do. We were witnesses, but powerless to prevent destruction. The bridge existed in theory, but not in practice."*

In southern Lebanon, civilians often viewed UN forces as distant, neutral observers—present, yet unable to ensure their safety. This duality exemplifies the limitations of the UN: it is both a stabilizer and a bystander, attempting to uphold peace while constrained by politics, mandates, and the realities of asymmetric warfare.

The Power of the Veto: When Politics Overrules Law

The UN Security Council's structure, particularly the veto power of its five permanent members—United States, Russia, China, France, and the United Kingdom—creates a paradox of authority. While the council has the ability to pass binding resolutions, a single veto can nullify international action, often leaving civilians unprotected.

During the Syrian civil war, for example, Russia repeatedly used its veto to block resolutions condemning Assad's regime or sanctioning attacks on civilians. The United States often pushed countermeasures that Moscow opposed, resulting in a stalemate. Diplomats debated endlessly in conference rooms far from the front lines, while families in Aleppo, Homs, and Idlib endured bombardments, sieges, and displacement.

Karim, a journalist reporting from Damascus in 2013, reflects: *"We watched reports from the UN. We saw statements, resolutions, and emergency sessions. But when the bombs fell on our streets, nothing changed. The bridge existed in theory, but in practice, it was a symbol, not a shield."*

The veto system illustrates a critical limitation of international law in practice: enforcement is contingent upon the interests of the most powerful members. When geopolitics trumps principle, the UN's legal frameworks become aspirational rather than operative, a bridge that can be withdrawn at any moment.

Humanitarian Aid and Refugee Protection

Beyond resolutions and peacekeeping, the UN operates through specialized agencies—UNHCR, UNICEF, and OCHA—to provide humanitarian aid and protection to vulnerable populations. Millions of refugees in Jordan, Lebanon, Iraq, and elsewhere rely on these agencies for food, shelter, education, and medical services.

Fatima, a Syrian refugee in a camp near Amman, recounts her experience: *"We sleep in tents. The children go to makeshift schools. There is food, sometimes enough. But we are waiting. Waiting for borders to open, for our homes to be rebuilt, for life to return. The UN helps, but it cannot rebuild our towns, our communities, or our futures."*

Even in these humanitarian interventions, the UN's bridge is narrow and incomplete. Its resources are limited, its mandates constrained, and its ability to enforce peace dependent on political backing. Aid may alleviate suffering, but it rarely addresses the root causes of conflict, leaving displaced communities suspended in limbo.

International Law: Compass Without Muscle

International law—comprising conventions, treaties, and UN resolutions—provides a framework intended to guide states toward peace, protect human rights, and prevent war crimes. The Geneva Conventions, the Convention on the Rights of the Child, and countless Security Council resolutions offer moral and legal guidance.

Yet in the Middle East, the application of these laws is uneven. Asymmetric warfare, airstrikes on civilian areas, and occupation blur the line between combatants and non-combatants. Legal norms debated in Geneva often fail to prevent suffering in Aleppo, Gaza, or Baghdad.

Human rights lawyer Nabil explains: *"International law is a compass. It tells you north, but it cannot move your feet for you. Governments and armed groups ignore it when it conflicts with their interests. For civilians, it is a book on a shelf while their lives burn."*

This disjunction underscores the central theme of *The Broken Bridge*: the UN's frameworks, while essential, are only partial bridges—they connect ideals, but often fail to reach the people most in need.

Case Studies: When Bridges Fail

Palestine: UN resolutions affirming Palestinian rights exist alongside ongoing expansion of settlements and military occupation. Humanitarian aid alleviates some suffering, but justice remains elusive.

Syria: Security Council resolutions condemning chemical attacks or mandating ceasefires are frequently vetoed or ignored. Peacekeeping missions cannot fully protect civilians.

Iraq: Sanctions and post-invasion resolutions shaped international engagement but often worsened civilian hardships, illustrating the gap between law and lived reality.

Yemen: Multiple UN resolutions have sought to halt the conflict, yet continued airstrikes, blockades, and famine reveal the limitations of enforcement.

These examples highlight a recurring truth: UN bridges are incomplete. They may span states, international institutions, and legal norms, but they rarely reach the civilians whose lives are most affected.

The Broken Bridge and the UN

The UN exemplifies both the **promise and limitations** of international intervention. It codifies norms, mediates disputes, and provides humanitarian support. Yet in a region shaped by colonial legacies, foreign interventions, authoritarian regimes, and persistent conflict, its mechanisms are often insufficient.

For political leaders, UN resolutions can confer legitimacy or diplomatic leverage. For civilians, however, the UN is often distant, symbolic, and fragile. Fatima in Jordan, Karim in Damascus, Amal in Ramallah—they all experience the UN as a witness, occasionally a protector, but rarely as an enforcer of justice or a restorer of their broken communities.

The United Nations' engagement in the Middle East is thus emblematic of *The Broken Bridge*: it is present, visible, and well-intentioned, yet fragile, incomplete, and often inaccessible to the people it is designed to protect. Its paper bridges connect states and institutions, but rarely the fractured human communities that lie beneath.

The United Nations and international law in the Middle East are bridges of principle and structure, attempting to connect conflict, injustice, and human suffering to accountability, protection, and resolution. Yet these bridges are partial, fragile, and politically constrained. Resolutions, vetoes, peacekeeping forces, and humanitarian aid provide moral and legal frameworks, but they do not guarantee safety, justice, or reconciliation.

For the ordinary citizens—the refugees, teachers, journalists, and aid workers—the UN remains a symbol of hope that often fails to translate into tangible protection. Like the other actors in this book—America, Russia, and China—the UN builds bridges across the region. But for all its ambition and moral authority, it struggles to span the deepest chasms of human suffering, political fragmentation, and historical grievances.

In the Middle East, the UN's bridges exist, but they are incomplete. They are frameworks without enforcement, promises without power, and structures without human reach. They are, ultimately, bridges of paper and principle, crossing rivers of conflict that continue to flow beneath, unbridged, and unhealed.

CHAPTER 3

THE HUMAN FACE OF WAR

War in the Middle East is not merely a sequence of battles, treaties, or military campaigns. It is a living, breathing catastrophe, etched into the faces of civilians, imprinted on the streets of ruined cities, and carried silently by generations who inherit its scars. Beyond the chessboard of superpowers and political maneuvering, the human consequences of decades-long conflict are staggering, and in many ways, permanent.

This chapter examines these human consequences in depth—exploring refugee crises, human rights violations, generational trauma, and environmental devastation. It is a journey into the lived realities of those whose lives have been defined by war, revealing the fractured human bridges that have left millions suspended between survival and despair.

Refugee Crises Across the Region

For millions, "home" is no longer a physical place but a memory, a story told in fragments, a photograph tucked into a backpack. Wars in Palestine, Syria, and Yemen have generated some of the largest refugee populations in modern history, stretching across borders and decades.

Palestine

The Palestinian refugee crisis is arguably the longest-standing in the modern world. In 1948, the Nakba—"catastrophe"—swept through Palestine, displacing hundreds of thousands of families. Villages were emptied, olive trees were burned, and entire communities vanished overnight. Today, generations later, Palestinian refugees still live in camps across Jordan, Lebanon, and the West Bank, trapped in a limbo between the past they never experienced and the future they may never reach.

Layla, a Palestinian nurse in Amman, grew up in the sprawling camp of Baqa'a:

"We were born in tents, went to school in makeshift classrooms, and dreamed of streets that didn't have barbed wire. My grandmother told stories of the olive trees she left behind in Haifa. Those trees became symbols for us—a reminder that home is somewhere out of reach. Even now, I walk the camp streets and hear my own children's laughter echoing against canvas walls. It's a kind of survival, but it is not life as it should be."

Despite decades of UN relief efforts—food distributions, health clinics, educational programs—Palestinian refugees endure chronic poverty, limited mobility, and political marginalization. They live on the margins of both host countries and international attention. Their lives are defined by waiting: waiting for aid, waiting for opportunity, waiting for a home that may never return.

Syria

The Syrian civil war, erupting in 2011, created one of the most acute humanitarian crises of the twenty-first century. Over 13 million people were displaced—internally or across borders—fleeing barrel bombs, chemical attacks, and the relentless grind of war. Camps in Jordan, Lebanon, and Turkey became temporary havens, yet even these "safe spaces" were fraught with scarcity, danger, and uncertainty.

Fatima, a Syrian mother of three, recalls the day she and her children fled Aleppo:

"We packed only what we could carry. I left behind my home, my neighbors, the market where my children played. When we crossed into Jordan, I realized that safety came with a price: we were strangers everywhere, dependent on aid that came irregularly, never enough. At night, my children cried, asking if we would ever go home. I had no answer. I could only hold them close and tell them we were alive."

The refugee crisis is far more than the physical act of displacement. It erodes normal life, childhood, and community cohesion. Children grow up without schools, families without livelihoods, and entire societies without stability. The human bridge of society—the network of intergenerational support, community, and belonging—is shattered, leaving millions suspended between survival and despair.

Yemen

In Yemen, conflict has compounded pre-existing vulnerabilities, creating a humanitarian crisis of immense scale. Hospitals lie in ruins, water is scarce, famine stalks the population, and disease, including cholera, has claimed thousands of lives. Refugees and internally displaced persons navigate a landscape where the borders of safety are constantly shifting, and where the next attack could come without warning.

Hassan, a fourteen-year-old boy displaced from Taiz, describes life in an internally displaced persons (IDP) camp:

"I wake up to dust, tents, and the smell of smoke from distant bombings. I dream of school, but my day is spent collecting water and helping my mother. The war is everywhere. Even when I close my eyes, it follows me. The only sound I trust is the call to prayer, because at least that reminds me there is something constant in this chaos."

In Yemen, like Syria and Palestine, the refugee crisis is not temporary—it is an enduring rupture, reshaping the very fabric of society. Lives are interrupted, childhoods stolen, and futures postponed indefinitely. Each displaced family is a testament to the human bridge that has been broken, one that will take decades, if not generations, to rebuild.

Human Rights Issues and War Crimes

The human cost of conflict is compounded by deliberate violations of human rights and the perpetration of war crimes. Across the region, civilians—men, women, and children—have been targeted or neglected in ways that violate international law.

In Syria, chemical attacks on civilians shocked the world, leaving neighborhoods in ruins and hospitals overwhelmed. Doctors, nurses, and ordinary citizens were often forced to become protectors and witnesses simultaneously.

Dr. Nabil, a pediatrician who fled Damascus, recounts:

"We treated children with burns, shrapnel wounds, and trauma. Sometimes, we would hear planes overhead, and I would tell the parents: get them under the table. One wrong step, one bombing, and everything was gone. We were medicine in a war that wanted to erase life."

In Yemen, airstrikes have destroyed markets, schools, and hospitals. International bodies may condemn these attacks, yet enforcement remains limited, leaving civilians to navigate a daily existence defined by fear and uncertainty.

Palestinian territories endure cycles of military occupation, restrictions on movement, arbitrary detention, and periodic escalations that result in civilian casualties. Rania, a human rights activist documenting abuses in Gaza, explains:

"We write reports, take photographs, speak to journalists. But the people on the ground continue to suffer. The law exists. The reports exist. But the bridge of justice never reaches them."

In these contexts, war is not simply a conflict between armies. It is a deliberate assault on civilian life, infrastructure, and the social fabric of communities—a violation of both human dignity and international law.

Generational Trauma: The Inheritance of War

War does not merely scar the present; it leaves a legacy of trauma that shapes the next generation. Children born into conflict inherit not only memories but fears, behaviors, and psychological burdens that will affect their entire lives.

Dr. Hadi, a psychologist working with refugee children in Syria and Palestine, explains:

"We see children with anxiety, nightmares, and aggression. They've never known normalcy. Their playgrounds are rubble. Their teachers are volunteers. They inherit fear—not only from what they witnessed but from what their parents lived through. Trauma becomes generational."

In Gaza, bombardments have destroyed neighborhoods, leaving children traumatized and schools in ruins. In Yemen, prolonged conflict combined with famine and disease has created a lost generation: children malnourished, uneducated, and psychologically burdened.

Generational trauma perpetuates instability. The human bridge between past and future is fractured, leaving a cycle of fear, displacement, and mistrust that extends well beyond the battlefield.

Environmental Damage of War

The consequences of war are not confined to human suffering. They seep into the soil, drift through the air, and poison the waters. Environmental destruction compounds the human cost, creating long-term challenges for survival and recovery. If war tears apart families, it also tears apart ecosystems. If it fractures societies, it also fractures the land itself. The environment, like people, becomes both a casualty and a witness.

Every bomb dropped, every factory shelled, every oil field set ablaze leaves a scar that outlasts ceasefires. Cities reduced to rubble, contaminated water supplies, scorched earth from bombing campaigns, and industrial pollution resulting from conflict all deepen the humanitarian crisis. These wounds, unlike broken buildings, cannot be repaired with bricks and cement alone. The healing of land requires decades, often longer than the span of human memory.

Syria: The Wounded Soil

In **Syria**, years of bombardment did not only demolish homes—it poisoned the earth itself. Bombed factories spilled chemicals into rivers and fields, transforming fertile valleys into wastelands. Aleppo, once famed for its olive groves and wheat fields, saw its agricultural heartlands scarred by toxic runoff. Hani, a farmer from the countryside, lamented what he had lost:

"We used to plant wheat, olives, and vegetables. Now the soil is poisoned. Even if the fighting ends tomorrow, the land may never recover. The earth itself is wounded, and with it, our hope for rebuilding."

In this testimony, the bridge between people and their land lies broken. The bond between farmer and field, miller and grain, community and harvest—fractured in ways invisible to those far from the soil. The war's toll will echo not only in ruined markets but in empty granaries for years to come.

Yemen: Water Turned Against the People

In **Yemen**, the war has weaponized water. Irrigation systems, once the veins of the land, have been shattered. Bombing campaigns damaged water treatment facilities; blockades prevented repair. Wells run dry or deliver water laced with disease. Cholera, an ancient plague, returned to Yemen not through natural misfortune but through human-made devastation.

Where once terraces on Yemen's mountainsides produced coffee, fruit, and sorghum, farmers now watch fields turn barren. The destruction of irrigation systems is not only the destruction of agriculture—it is the unraveling of community life itself. The bridge between the Yemeni people and their sustenance has snapped, leaving children to grow up in famine not of nature's making, but of war's design.

Palestine: The Severed Roots of the Olive Tree

In **Palestine**, olive trees stand as more than crops—they are symbols of resilience, belonging, and continuity. Some trees are hundreds of years old, planted by ancestors whose names are long forgotten, yet whose labor still feeds families today.

The destruction of olive groves is more than an economic blow; it severs cultural roots. Each felled tree is a broken memory, each uprooted grove a denial of heritage. For families who gathered under these trees for harvest, meals, and celebrations, the loss is deeply personal. The olive tree, slow to grow and slower to replace, reminds us that the destruction of the environment is also the destruction of time itself. When the tree falls, generations fall with it.

Iran: The Hidden Scars of an Older War

In **Iran**, the scars of war run deep into the land, often hidden beneath the surface. During the Iran–Iraq War of the 1980s, oil fields were set ablaze, darkening skies with smoke and saturating soil with toxins. The marshlands of Khuzestan, once rich in biodiversity, were drained or polluted during years of conflict. Entire ecosystems collapsed, and with them, the livelihoods of fishing and farming communities who depended on these waters.

Perhaps most haunting are the landmines. Decades after the ceasefire, farmers in Khuzestan and along the western border still risk their lives planting crops. Vast fields remain unplowed, not for lack of soil but for fear of hidden explosives. Each mine is an invisible reminder that the earth, too, remembers war. It holds danger in silence, waiting underfoot.

The younger generation, born long after the war ended, still lives with its consequences. For them, the bridge to the land remains incomplete. They cannot plant freely, cannot trust their own soil, cannot reclaim the marshes their grandparents once fished. Their inheritance is not fertile ground but a terrain laced with danger.

Environmental damage, like generational trauma, ensures that war's consequences extend far beyond the battlefield. A city can be rebuilt, but poisoned soil may take decades to heal. A child can return to school, but water polluted by chemicals may remain undrinkable for generations. Forests do not grow back overnight; aquifers do not cleanse themselves on command. The earth moves slowly, carrying the memory of war long after humans try to forget.

The broken bridge of the environment is perhaps the hardest to repair. Unlike treaties, it cannot be signed into existence. Unlike governments, it cannot be overthrown or elected. The land demands patience, science, resources, and above all, recognition—that the earth itself must be treated as a casualty of war.

To heal the land is to heal the people. Fields cleared of mines, rivers restored to health, groves replanted, and marshes revived—these are not luxuries, but essentials for recovery. For without them, no society can rebuild fully. A people cut off from their environment is a people stranded on one side of the bridge, unable to reach the future that awaits on the other.

The Broken Bridge and the Human Cost

Across the Middle East, the consequences of war are profound, personal, and enduring. Refugees walk paths of displacement, children carry inherited trauma, communities navigate destroyed infrastructure, and the environment bears the scars of decades-long conflict.

Even with humanitarian aid, human rights organizations, and international intervention, the bridges that connect civilians to safety, justice, and recovery remain fragile, partial, or absent. For Fatima, Layla, and Hassan, life is a suspended journey—a daily negotiation between survival and despair.

The human face of war is the clearest evidence of the broken bridge of humanities in the Middle East: between people and safety, between generations and normalcy, and between communities and the land that sustains them. It is a reminder that while political negotiations, military interventions, and international resolutions may dominate headlines, the true cost of conflict is lived by ordinary people.

The human consequences of war—refugee crises, human rights violations, generational trauma, and environmental destruction— reveal the profound failure of broken bridge of humanities across the Middle East. The region's people inherit the legacy of conflict in both visible and invisible scars, struggling daily to survive while international actors attempt, often inadequately, to intervene.

To comprehend the Middle East is to witness this broken bridge of humanity's: shattered communities, lost childhoods, scarred lands, and displaced populations. The human face of war is both a testament to resilience and a somber reminder of the deep fractures that continue to shape the region. Rebuilding these bridges requires more than diplomacy or aid; it demands an engagement with the lived realities of war's victims and the moral courage to restore what has been destroyed.

Human Rights Issues and War Crimes

The Middle East has, for decades, been a theater of widespread human rights violations and war crimes. Beyond the headlines of military campaigns, international summits, and resolutions, the human cost of conflict is carried by civilians—men, women, and children whose lives are torn apart by deliberate violations of law and morality. These are acts not merely of chance in the chaos of war, but often intentional strategies: hospitals bombed, neighborhoods shelled, civilians used as shields. The human consequences are immediate, long-lasting, and intergenerational.

Syria: Chemical Attacks and the Siege of Civilians

In Syria, the civil war that erupted in 2011 has been characterized by brutality that shocked the global conscience. Chemical attacks on civilian populations, indiscriminate bombings, and sieges of cities such as Aleppo and Ghouta have left entire neighborhoods in ruins, hospitals nonfunctional, and healthcare workers forced into impossible moral dilemmas.

Dr. Nabil, a pediatrician who fled Damascus, remembers the horrors he witnessed:

"We treated children with burns, shrapnel wounds, and trauma. Sometimes, we would hear planes overhead, and I would tell the parents: get them under the table. One wrong step, one bombing, and everything was gone. We were medicine in a war that wanted to erase life."

He recalls nights when families would huddle in basements, listening to bombs shake the walls above them. Hospitals became targets rather than sanctuaries, and ambulances navigating the streets risked being struck at any moment. For Dr. Nabil and his colleagues, survival meant improvisation: treating wounds with minimal supplies, relocating patients constantly, and witnessing the trauma of children who would never see a world without fear.

Chemical attacks, particularly the sarin gas assault on Ghouta in 2013, are emblematic of war crimes in the Syrian conflict. Entire families were killed or maimed in minutes. International condemnation was swift, yet enforcement and accountability were limited. These attacks underscored the grim reality: international laws exist, but without political will and enforcement, they remain paper shields against live-fire brutality.

Yemen: The Human Toll of Airstrikes and Blockades

In Yemen, the humanitarian catastrophe is compounded by a combination of armed conflict, airstrikes, and blockades that prevent food, medicine, and essential supplies from reaching civilians. airstrikes have destroyed markets, schools, hospitals, and water infrastructure, leaving millions vulnerable to disease, malnutrition, and displacement.

Hassan, a fifteen-year-old displaced from Taiz, recounts the terror of daily life:

"The sky screams before we even see the planes. One day, our school was hit. Books, walls, children—everything collapsed. My friends were buried under the rubble. Even if we survive, we are marked forever by what we saw."

International bodies issue condemnations and humanitarian appeals, yet enforcement is limited. War crimes—airstrikes on civilian infrastructure, indiscriminate shelling, and attacks on humanitarian convoys—often go unpunished. For families on the ground, accountability feels like a distant promise. For Hassan and countless others, survival is immediate; justice is abstract.

Palestine: Occupation, Blockades, and Cycles of Violence

Palestinian territories—Gaza, the West Bank, and East Jerusalem—experience a different, yet equally devastating, pattern of human rights violations. Military occupation, restrictions on movement, arbitrary detention, home demolitions, and periodic escalations of violence create a chronic humanitarian crisis.

Rania, a human rights activist documenting abuses in Gaza, describes her work:

"We write reports, take photographs, and speak to journalists. But the people on the ground continue to suffer. The law exists, the reports exist, but the bridge of justice never reaches them. Children grow up knowing checkpoints, tanks, and tear gas as constants. When they play, the fear is always present."

Palestinian civilians endure a slow-burning violence: food insecurity, limited access to healthcare, and periodic military campaigns that leave neighborhoods in ruins. These violations, while not always classified as conventional "war crimes," reflect systemic breaches of human rights that have persisted for decades.

Iraq: A Landscape of Collateral Damage

Iraq presents yet another dimension. The 2003 invasion, followed by sectarian violence, insurgencies, and campaigns against ISIS, created an environment where civilians were repeatedly caught in crossfire. Bombings, chemical exposure, mass executions, and targeted killings created a pervasive climate of fear. Human rights organizations documented atrocities on all sides, yet many perpetrators remained unaccountable, and survivors were left to rebuild amidst rubble and trauma.

Amir, a young man from Mosul, recounts:

"We buried neighbors in our backyard. Schools were rubble. Hospitals were empty. We were left to survive without guidance, protection, or justice. Even when the violence ended, life did not return—it only changed shape. The bridge from law to life had collapsed completely."

The Limits of International Law and Enforcement

Across Syria, Yemen, Palestine, and Iraq, human rights violations persist despite international conventions, tribunals, and UN resolutions. The Geneva Conventions, the International Criminal Court, and Security Council resolutions create a framework for accountability, but political interests, veto powers, and enforcement gaps often render these instruments ineffective.

This reality underscores the central theme of The Broken Bridge: laws, resolutions, and international mandates are bridges meant to protect civilians and prevent atrocities—but in practice, they are often incomplete, fragile, or blocked by political realities. Civilians remain stranded in conflict zones, while the mechanisms of justice exist only in theory.

Voices from the Ground

The language of war often hides its reality. International reports speak of "escalations," "operations," and "violations." Governments debate resolutions and hold press conferences. But for those who live in the shadow of war, these words are hollow. On the ground, people know war not as policy but as hunger, fear, and grief. Their voices remind us that when the bridges of law and morality collapse, it is ordinary civilians who fall into the void.

In **Syria**, a mother sits among the rubble of Aleppo. Her voice is quiet, steady, but edged with exhaustion:

"We pray that the world sees us, but the world sees papers, votes, and cameras. We see ruins, blood, and loss."

She does not speak of strategy or ideology. She speaks of absence—the absence of shelter, of protection, of anyone to hear her cries above the noise of global debate. The bridge of international solidarity, she feels, has long since broken.

In **Yemen**, a doctor walks through the hushed halls of a damaged hospital. His words carry the weary authority of someone who has seen too much:

"Our ambulances are targets. Our patients are statistics in someone else's debate."

For him, the bridge of medical neutrality—once a cornerstone of humanitarian law—has collapsed. The red crescent on his ambulance no longer offers protection. Every journey is a gamble, every patient a reminder of promises broken by the world outside.

In **Palestine**, a teacher gathers her students in a crowded classroom. The walls are cracked, the electricity unreliable, yet she insists on beginning each lesson with a discussion of rights and justice. Later, she confides:

"We teach children about rights, freedom, and justice—but every day, they experience the opposite. The law is a story told somewhere else."

Her words expose another broken bridge—the one meant to connect law to life. For her students, rights remain concepts in a textbook, never lived realities.

And in **Israel**, a young father recalls the night sirens pierced the air and he rushed his family to a shelter. His daughter, clutching his hand, looked up with frightened eyes:

"I hold my daughter's hand and tell her it will be okay, but the truth is I don't know. She asks why the sky is dangerous. I have no answer."

Here the broken bridge is one of safety. For him, protection means walls of concrete and reinforced steel doors. But even these cannot shield his daughter from fear—the kind that seeps into childhood, shaping how she will see the world.

These voices—Syrian, Yemeni, Palestinian, Israeli—do not accuse. They testify. They remind us that beneath political divisions lies a shared human truth: the desire for dignity, safety, and peace. When bridges collapse—whether of law, morality, or humanity—it is not leaders or generals who fall, but mothers, teachers, doctors, and children.

The metaphor of the broken bridge takes on flesh here. It is not just a concept. It is the cracked classroom wall, the poisoned well, the air-raid siren, the empty field where olives once grew. To rebuild these bridges means more than treaties or ceasefires. It means restoring trust that the world will see civilians not as footnotes to conflict but as the center of it.

The Broken Bridge: Human Rights and War Crimes

Human rights violations and war crimes in the Middle East illustrate the profound fragility of bridges intended to protect human life. Across Syria, Yemen, Palestine, and Iraq, civilians endure suffering because accountability is limited, enforcement is inconsistent, and international law often clashes with political expediency.

The broken bridge of humanity manifests in physical destruction, psychological trauma, displacement, and intergenerational fear. The very institutions designed to protect human life—the UN, the ICC, humanitarian organizations—often struggle to reach those most in need. For survivors, the gap between law and lived reality is the most devastating: a bridge that exists on paper but fails to carry the weight of human suffering.

In this way, the human cost of war is not only measured in lives lost or cities destroyed—it is measured in broken promises, absent protections, and the enduring vulnerability of those who have nowhere to turn. It is the human face of The Broken Bridge, a testament to the region's ongoing struggle to reconcile violence with justice, survival with dignity, and law with life.

Generational Trauma: The Inheritance of War

War does not simply end when the last bomb falls or when ceasefires are declared. Its echoes ripple across time, shaping the lives of children, families, and communities for decades. In the Middle East, decades of conflict—from Palestine to Syria, Yemen to Iraq—have left behind not only physical destruction but an invisible inheritance: trauma. This trauma is carried silently across generations, molding behaviors, fears, and relationships, and shaping the very foundations of society.

In the cities, villages, and camps that have borne the brunt of conflict, children grow up amid ruins. Their playgrounds are rubble; their schools are makeshift tents or damaged buildings; their futures are uncertain. They inherit not only stories of loss but the psychological burdens of those who survived the wars before them. In this chapter, we trace these inherited traumas, explore the coping strategies that allow survival, examine community-based resilience, and reflect on how these lessons shape young generations.

The Visible and Invisible Scars

Trauma manifests in ways that are immediately visible and deeply hidden. In Gaza, children navigate streets lined with shell-shattered buildings. Windows are broken, walls scorched, and balconies bent from repeated airstrikes. For them, normalcy is a memory told by parents, grandparents, or older siblings.

Ahmed, a ten-year-old in Gaza, explains:

"I wake up and look outside. The sky is clear, but I listen for planes. At school, I draw houses and markets, but my house is broken. At night, explosions follow me into my dreams."

In Yemen, children face compounded adversity. The combination of war, famine, and disease has created a lost generation: malnourished, uneducated, and psychologically burdened. Hassan, a fourteen-year-old from Taiz, recalls:

"We wake to dust, tents, and the smell of smoke. I dream of school, but my day is collecting water and helping my mother. The war is everywhere. Even when I close my eyes, it follows."

Syria presents yet another dimension. During the siege of Aleppo, neighborhoods were flattened. Hospitals became targets. Families were forced into basements to survive, and children watched the death of neighbors, teachers, and friends. These experiences create invisible scars—an inheritance of fear and hypervigilance that parents transmit, consciously or not, to their children.

Dr. Hadi, a psychologist working with refugee children in Syria and Palestine, observes:

"Trauma becomes generational. Children inherit fear—not only from what they witness but from what their parents lived through. Their brains learn to anticipate danger even in moments of calm. It's an invisible inheritance that shapes who they are."

Coping Strategies: Survival in a Fractured World

Even amid chaos, children and families develop strategies to cope. For some, it is the establishment of routines: waking at a certain hour, attending school, helping siblings, or participating in chores. For others, it is creative expression: drawing, storytelling, or music becomes a lifeline in environments defined by fear.

Sami, fifteen, a Syrian refugee in Jordan, explains:

"I wake up early, help my little brother, go to school. At school, I am normal for a few hours. I forget the bombs. I forget the nights we ran."

Storytelling, often through informal narratives passed down in families, helps preserve identity and cultural continuity. Fatima, a mother in a Yemen IDP camp, recounts:

"I tell my children stories of our ancestors, of courage and survival. The war is hidden in my stories, but strength runs in our veins. It comforts them. It comforts me."

Art therapy and creative workshops organized by NGOs provide structured outlets for children. In Gaza, youth participate in painting sessions where they reconstruct their lost neighborhoods on paper, imagining a city rebuilt not by governments or aid, but by their own hands. These exercises help children reclaim agency over their narratives, countering feelings of helplessness and despair.

Community-Based Healing: Collective Resilience

While individual coping is vital, community-based healing offers a deeper form of resilience. In Palestinian refugee camps in Lebanon, youth centers, cultural programs, and vocational workshops provide spaces where children regain a sense of normalcy and social cohesion. In Syria, neighborhood networks rotate caregiving responsibilities, share resources, and organize small cultural or religious events to preserve a sense of continuity.

Even in Yemen, informal educational programs combine literacy and psychosocial support. Children learn, play, and process trauma collectively. These networks foster trust, cooperation, and social bonds, creating a fragile but vital bridge to a sense of stability and hope.

Dr. Hadi emphasizes:

"Communities are remarkably resilient. Healing is not always formal—it is embedded in daily acts of care, sharing, and cultural preservation. These acts form the skeleton of bridges that war seeks to destroy."

Historical Context: Trauma Across Decades

Generational trauma in the Middle East is not an isolated phenomenon. It is rooted in decades of conflict that have repeatedly fractured families and societies. Palestinian children inherit displacement and occupation dating back to 1948. Lebanese communities carry the legacy of a fifteen-year civil war. Iraq's population endured the Iran-Iraq War, the Gulf War, the U.S. invasion in 2003, and ISIS occupation. Syria's civil war is the most recent iteration in a long history of instability.

This historical accumulation of trauma means children inherit more than immediate fear—they inherit collective memory, unresolved grief, and mistrust of institutions. Families raise children amid ongoing instability, creating an intergenerational cycle of stress, anxiety, and vigilance.

Longitudinal Effects: Education, Employment, and Social Cohesion

The inheritance of trauma has lasting consequences:

Education: War disrupts schooling. Schools are destroyed, teachers flee, curricula are interrupted. Psychological trauma impairs concentration, memory, and social skills, leading to lower academic achievement and limiting future opportunities.

Employment: Adolescents entering adulthood often lack skills and confidence, reinforcing cycles of poverty and marginalization. Economic instability perpetuates psychological stress, further fracturing families and communities.

Social Cohesion: Communities fractured by violence struggle to trust neighbors, engage in civic life, or rebuild governance. Trauma shapes relationships, erodes trust, and delays societal reconciliation.

Rania, a Palestinian teacher, notes:

"Our children are smart, creative, and resilient, but they carry fear like a second skin. That fear influences how they work, parent, and participate in society. Trauma is a legacy that changes communities."

Lessons Learned and the Path Forward

Despite these challenges, generational trauma offers critical lessons:

The Fragility of Safety: Young generations understand that security is not guaranteed. They learn to anticipate risk, a skill that fosters caution but can also breed mistrust.

The Power of Community: Children learn resilience through shared experience. Networks of mutual support are vital in rebuilding trust and social cohesion.

Memory as Identity: Storytelling, art, and cultural preservation transmit history and identity, helping children process trauma and maintain dignity.

Addressing generational trauma requires long-term investment in mental health, education, and community cohesion. Immediate relief—food, shelter, medical aid—is insufficient. Psychological and social interventions are essential to prevent the perpetuation of fear, mistrust, and instability.

Programs that integrate vocational training, psychosocial support, and creative expression help youth reclaim agency. By nurturing resilience, we equip young generations not only to survive but to rebuild the bridges destroyed by decades of conflict.

Hope Amidst the Rubble

Generational trauma is a profound challenge, but it also offers a paradoxical opportunity. Children growing up amid conflict develop empathy, adaptability, and resourcefulness. Their inherited experiences, if supported with care and investment, can cultivate leaders, community builders, and advocates for peace.

Fatima, a young Yemeni mother, reflects:

"We survived the bombs, the hunger, the fear. Our children will inherit our scars—but they can also inherit our courage. That is the bridge we hope to leave them: a bridge strong enough to carry them beyond the war we endured."

The broken bridge of humanitys of the Middle East are not only physical—they are social, psychological, and moral. Healing requires attention to the invisible fractures as much as the visible ones. By supporting the mental, emotional, and social well-being of children and young adults, we begin to reconstruct what war has broken.

The task is immense. Generational trauma is pervasive, interwoven with history, culture, and politics. But the resilience, courage, and creativity of young generations offer a pathway forward. With sustained investment in communities, education, and healing, the bridges of tomorrow can rise from the rubble of yesterday.

Dr. Hadi concludes with cautious optimism:

"The children we work with today carry the scars of history—but they also carry the seeds of change. If we invest in their healing, we are not just repairing bridges broken by war; we are building bridges to a future that might finally stand."

Environmental Damage of War: The Scars on Land, Water, and Life

War is often measured in human casualties, territorial gains, or political headlines, yet another, less immediately visible cost lingers long after the ceasefires and treaties: the environment itself. In the Middle East, decades of conflict—from Palestine and Syria to Yemen and Iraq—have left deep ecological scars. Rivers poisoned, farmland destroyed, air thick with toxins, and cities left in rubble are only the beginning. The environmental consequences of war ripple through communities, agriculture, water systems, and health, creating a persistent legacy that further fractures societies and deepens the broken bridge of humanitys of human life.

Cities as Rubble, Soil as Ash

The physical destruction of urban centers is the most visible form of environmental damage. In Aleppo, once a city of bustling markets, narrow streets, and ancient stone buildings, decades of bombing have flattened neighborhoods. Rubble piles line the streets, not only burying homes but releasing dust and particulate matter into the air.

Hanan, a Syrian mother, recalls:

"Our apartment was gone. The building next door was rubble. We could not open the windows without choking on dust. My children cough constantly. Even after the war, the city feels sick."

This rubble is not inert—it seeps toxins into the soil. Lead from destroyed batteries, asbestos from damaged roofs, and chemicals from shattered industrial facilities contaminate urban soil. For children playing amid the ruins, the environment itself becomes hazardous. War leaves cities not only uninhabitable but slowly toxic, posing long-term health risks.

Water Scarcity and Pollution

Water is life in the Middle East, yet conflict has repeatedly turned rivers and aquifers into vectors of disease. In Yemen, airstrikes have damaged water treatment facilities, leaving millions dependent on untreated, contaminated sources. Cholera outbreaks have surged, compounded by famine and malnutrition, as families struggle to find even a single liter of safe water.

Sami, a twelve-year-old in a Taiz IDP camp, explains:

"We walk for hours to collect water. Sometimes it smells funny, sometimes it makes us sick. We are careful, but we always drink. There is no choice."

In Syria, rivers like the Euphrates and the Orontes have been affected by bombed dams, chemical runoff, and disrupted irrigation networks. Farms once relied upon feeding communities now produce less, not only because of lost labor but because the land itself is poisoned. Agriculture collapses under the weight of war, forcing displacement, hunger, and economic instability.

Air and Soil Contamination

Airborne toxins are another silent consequence of war. Explosions release smoke, heavy metals, and fine particulate matter into the air, creating respiratory hazards. In Gaza, repeated shelling and urban conflict have led to increased asthma, chronic cough, and other respiratory ailments among children.

Soil contamination is equally insidious. In Iraq, conflicts have left behind oil spills, burned chemical stockpiles, and unexploded ordnance scattered across farmland. This contamination reduces agricultural yield, poisons livestock, and limits access to safe food, creating a vicious cycle of environmental and human vulnerability.

Fatima, a farmer near Basra, recounts:

"Our fields are black with oil. Crops grow, but they taste bitter. Some of our sheep died after grazing near the river. We try, but the land is sick. The war has not only taken our homes but our earth."

Forests, Biodiversity, and Ecosystems

War also decimates forests, wetlands, and wildlife. In Syria, forest fires resulting from shelling have destroyed centuries-old trees and displaced wildlife. In Yemen, overgrazing and deforestation accelerated by conflict exacerbate desertification. Biodiversity suffers as habitats shrink and water scarcity intensifies.

Communities that once depended on these ecosystems—herders, farmers, and fishermen—find their livelihoods threatened. The environmental destruction compounds social and economic instability, perpetuating cycles of poverty and displacement.

Climate Vulnerability and Long-Term Consequences

The Middle East is already vulnerable to climate change. Prolonged droughts, rising temperatures, and unpredictable rainfall patterns are now intensified by war-induced environmental damage. Destruction of infrastructure, contaminated water, and depleted agricultural land make communities less resilient to climate shocks.

For displaced families, climate stress compounds trauma. Camps in Jordan, Lebanon, and Yemen suffer from heatwaves, scarce water, and poor sanitation. The environment becomes another adversary, threatening survival even where human violence has temporarily receded.

Human Stories Amid Environmental Collapse

Environmental degradation is inseparable from human suffering. Children inhale dust from crumbling buildings; women fetch water from polluted wells; farmers watch as poisoned soil yields no crops. War's ecological toll is intimately tied to the human face of conflict.

Rashid, a Palestinian father in Gaza, explains:

"The war took my home. Then it took our streets, our water, our gardens. My children cough every day. Even if the fighting stops, we live among sickness and dust. The bridge to a normal life is broken not only by bombs but by the land itself."

In Yemen, children carry water and food from distant sources. Adults worry not only about airstrikes but about cholera, malnutrition, and crop failure. Environmental collapse exacerbates human vulnerability, prolonging trauma and undermining recovery.

The Broken Bridge and Environmental Damage

The environmental destruction wrought by war is another form of broken bridge of humanity. Just as cities, families, and communities are fractured, the land itself—the foundation of life and stability—is shattered. Rebuilding cannot only focus on infrastructure or politics; it must address the ecological scars that undermine survival, health, and social cohesion.

Reconstruction efforts often prioritize human shelter and economic recovery while neglecting the environment. Yet, without soil restoration, water purification, and ecosystem rehabilitation, communities remain trapped in cycles of vulnerability and displacement. The environment, like society, must be healed to restore the bridges that conflict has broken.

Toward Environmental Recovery and Hope

Amid destruction, there are glimmers of renewal. In Syria, small community-driven initiatives plant trees in destroyed neighborhoods. In Yemen, NGOs install solar water pumps to reduce reliance on contaminated wells. Palestinian farmers experiment with rooftop gardens, hydroponics, and rainwater harvesting to reclaim agricultural resilience.

These efforts demonstrate that environmental restoration is not just about ecology—it is about rebuilding lives, communities, and human potential. Healing the land creates spaces where children can play safely, families can farm, and societies can regain stability.

Hanan, the Syrian mother, reflects:

"We clear the rubble. We plant seeds. My children see green again. For the first time in years, they laugh without fear. The bridge is not gone—it is just under repair."

War's Environmental Legacy

The environmental consequences of war in the Middle East are deep, pervasive, and long-lasting. Soil, water, air, and ecosystems bear the weight of conflict, just as people do. These scars exacerbate human suffering, perpetuate cycles of displacement, and threaten the recovery of communities already fractured by violence.

Addressing environmental damage is essential to rebuilding the bridges broken by war. Restoring water systems, rehabilitating farmland, cleaning soil, and replanting forests are not just ecological acts—they are acts of social, economic, and moral reconstruction.

The environment, like society, carries the legacy of war—but with deliberate attention, care, and sustained effort, it can also be a source of hope. Children can grow up breathing clean air, drinking safe water, and walking on fertile soil. Communities can rebuild livelihoods. And the broken bridge of humanity's between human beings, and between people and the land, can begin to heal.

CHAPTER 4

Pathways to Peace

Rebuilding the Broken Bridges

The Middle East has endured decades of conflict, leaving cities in rubble, communities uprooted, and generations scarred by trauma. From the burned-out streets of Aleppo and Gaza to the famine-stricken valleys of Yemen, the human cost of war is visible not only in physical destruction but in the silent burdens carried by survivors. Families live in displacement camps, children grow up amid checkpoints and ruins, and communities struggle to maintain social cohesion while violence, mistrust, and despair permeate daily life. The scars of war are not merely structural—they are moral, psychological, and deeply social, affecting the way individuals relate to one another and imagine a shared future.

Amid this devastation, hope is fragile but persistent. In the ruins of bombed-out neighborhoods, grassroots organizations rebuild schools, health clinics, and community centers. In refugee camps, women organize educational programs, vocational training, and cultural activities to restore a sense of normalcy. Young people, though raised amid fear and instability, envision lives beyond the rubble, seeking opportunities for education, dialogue, and civic engagement. These efforts, often overlooked by policymakers or the international media, represent the first bricks in the reconstruction of societal bridges— bridges of trust, dignity, and community cohesion.

Rebuilding society in the Middle East requires more than ending violence or negotiating ceasefires. It demands addressing the deeper fractures left by decades of conflict: the erosion of social trust, the perpetuation of trauma across generations, and the breakdown of moral and civic structures that once bound communities together. Peace cannot be measured solely by the absence of bombs or the signing of political agreements; it must be measured by the ability of individuals and communities to coexist, cooperate, and envision a shared future. In essence, peace is the reconstruction of human bridges—social, moral, and psychological—that connect people to one another and to the broader society.

Drawing lessons from other societies that have endured deep divisions provides both inspiration and guidance. South Africa emerged from apartheid through truth-telling, acknowledgment of past injustices, and structured reconciliation, offering a model for addressing historical grievances and rebuilding moral trust. Rwanda confronted neighbor-on-neighbor violence through community-based courts and grassroots restorative justice, demonstrating the power of local engagement in mending fractured relationships. Northern Ireland, after decades of sectarian violence, relied on persistent negotiation, inclusive dialogue, and long-term confidence-building measures to stabilize communities and foster coexistence.

While these examples are not perfect analogs for the Middle East—with its overlapping conflicts, foreign interventions, and ongoing crises—they highlight enduring principles: truth, justice, reconciliation, and community engagement are essential for any durable peace. These principles must be adapted to local contexts, sensitive to cultural norms, historical grievances, and existing social dynamics. They must also account for the lived realities of civilians who carry the legacies of war in their bodies, minds, and communities.

Central to any sustainable peace in the Middle East are the empowerment of women and the inclusion of youth. Women, who often bear the primary responsibility for family and community survival amid conflict, are essential architects of social cohesion, capable of restoring educational, health, and cultural structures. Youth, who inherit both the trauma and the potential of their societies, are critical for sustaining peace over the long term, ensuring that bridges are not only rebuilt but strengthened for future generations.

Ultimately, the pursuit of peace is not a political exercise alone; it is a deeply human endeavor. It requires the acknowledgment of suffering, the cultivation of empathy, and the construction of bridges that carry moral and social weight. In the Middle East, these bridges are not physical structures alone but represent networks of trust, understanding, and shared responsibility—a reconstruction of society that honors both the past and the promise of the future. Rebuilding these bridges is slow, deliberate, and often painful, but it is the only path toward a region where children can grow beyond the shadows of war, where communities can coexist without fear, and where hope can finally take root.

South Africa: Truth, Reconciliation, and the Moral Bridge

South Africa's transition from apartheid to democracy is widely regarded as one of the most significant experiments in restorative justice in modern history. After decades of institutionalized racial oppression, segregation, and systematic violence, the country faced a monumental task: reconciling deeply divided communities, addressing the atrocities committed by both the apartheid state and resistance movements, and laying the foundations for a democratic society. Central to this process was the creation of the Truth and Reconciliation Commission (TRC), a body that became a moral and social bridge between the past and the future.

The TRC was structured around the principle that healing begins with acknowledgment. Perpetrators of human rights abuses were given an opportunity to confess their actions in exchange for conditional amnesty, while victims were provided a public platform to recount the suffering they endured. Importantly, the TRC was not designed solely to deliver legal punishment; it was designed to restore human dignity and rebuild social trust. It recognized that justice is not only about punishment, but also about acknowledgment, understanding, and the reconstruction of moral bonds within society.

For the Middle East, this model provides profound lessons. Decades of conflict in the region have left communities deeply fractured. In countries like Syria, Yemen, Iraq, and Palestine, neighbors have been turned against one another, families have been displaced, and social cohesion has been eroded. The principle embedded in the TRC—that truth-telling and acknowledgment of suffering are prerequisites for rebuilding trust—can be adapted to these contexts. Public acknowledgment of atrocities and historical injustices, whether through national commissions, local community forums, or educational initiatives, creates a space for moral accountability and collective healing. Truth-telling becomes not merely a historical record but a form of bridge-building, reconnecting fractured communities by confronting the past rather than ignoring or suppressing it.

Moreover, South Africa's experience illustrates the essential interdependence of truth and justice. While acknowledgment of past wrongs is necessary, it cannot function in isolation. A society cannot sustain peace if victims feel ignored, if perpetrators act with impunity, or if justice appears selective or incomplete. In the Middle East, mechanisms for truth must be paired with systems of accountability. Courts, hybrid tribunals, or community-based restorative justice processes can provide the necessary legal and social framework to prevent cycles of grievance and revenge from perpetuating conflict. Without this balance, truth-telling risks being symbolic rather than transformative.

The South African model also demonstrates the power of transparency, participation, and societal engagement in reconciliation. The TRC conducted public hearings that were broadcast across the country, ensuring that the process was visible and accessible. Communities were not passive observers; they were participants in the moral reconstruction of society. This approach underscores the idea that reconciliation cannot be imposed from the top down—it must involve citizens in meaningful ways, creating a shared sense of responsibility and ownership over the peacebuilding process.

Importantly, the TRC also addressed the psychological and moral dimensions of healing. By providing a forum for victims' stories and fostering acknowledgment from perpetrators, it recognized the human need for validation, empathy, and understanding. Healing was framed not only as a legal or political necessity but as a moral imperative, an acknowledgment that human dignity must be restored before society as a whole can move forward.

Translating these lessons to the Middle East requires adaptation to local realities. While ongoing conflicts, foreign interventions, and political fragmentation make a South Africa-style TRC challenging to replicate fully, the underlying principles remain relevant. Initiatives could include community-level truth commissions, regional acknowledgment forums, educational curricula that incorporate narratives of suffering and resilience, and mechanisms that integrate moral acknowledgment with legal accountability. Each of these initiatives can serve as a stepping stone in reconstructing the broken bridges of trust, dignity, and social cohesion that decades of war have eroded.

Ultimately, South Africa's example demonstrates that peace is more than a political settlement or cessation of hostilities. It is a moral endeavor, a reconstruction of human relationships fractured by historical injustice. Truth, when coupled with justice and community engagement, becomes a bridge—connecting individuals, communities, and generations, and offering a foundation on which sustainable peace can be built. For the Middle East, where histories of conflict are long and complex, this approach offers both a framework and a moral imperative: societies must confront their past to reclaim a future built on trust, dignity, and shared humanity.

Truth, Justice, and Reconciliation in the Middle East Context

The concept of truth, justice, and reconciliation (TJR) has been applied in societies emerging from conflict across the globe, from South Africa to Rwanda, to address the moral, social, and political wounds left by prolonged violence. In the Middle East, however, the implementation of such mechanisms is uniquely challenging. Unlike South Africa, where apartheid had formally ended, or Rwanda, where the genocide was a discrete, albeit devastating, historical event, the Middle East faces ongoing wars, foreign occupations, and overlapping internal conflicts that fragment authority and complicate the pursuit of accountability. Displacement is widespread, with millions living as refugees or internally displaced persons, and political structures are often weak or contested.

Despite these obstacles, the principles of TJR remain crucial. They provide a moral framework for addressing human suffering, rebuilding social cohesion, and fostering durable peace. While implementation must be adapted to local realities, the underlying goal is consistent:

to restore human dignity, prevent cycles of violence, and reconstruct bridges—both social and moral—that have been shattered by decades of conflict.

Truth: Documenting and Acknowledging Suffering

Truth is the foundation of reconciliation. It involves creating safe and credible avenues for survivors to recount their experiences, ensuring that their suffering is acknowledged, recorded, and remembered. In the Middle East, truth-telling would encompass multiple layers of experience: Palestinian refugees living in camps across Jordan, Lebanon, and the West Bank; Syrian civilians who survived bombings, sieges, and chemical attacks; Yemeni families navigating famine, disease, and airstrikes; and countless others whose lives have been shaped by conflict.

Truth-telling mechanisms could include historical documentation projects, local and regional forums, educational programs, or international platforms. The key is to create spaces where survivors' stories are validated and preserved, forming a collective record that acknowledges both individual and communal trauma. Beyond documentation, these narratives serve a social purpose: they humanize victims, contextualize violence, and provide a moral counterweight to political or military narratives that often obscure human suffering.

Implementing truth in the Middle East is not without challenges. Fear of retaliation, political instability, and the fragmentation of communities often inhibit public testimony. Nevertheless, even partial or localized truth-telling initiatives—community-led storytelling projects, memorialization efforts, or archival programs—can serve as starting points for moral acknowledgment and social reconstruction. By recognizing the lived experiences of those most affected, societies begin to restore the human bridges that conflict has eroded.

Justice: Accountability to Prevent Impunity

Truth alone is insufficient. Without accountability, the acknowledgment of suffering risks being symbolic rather than transformative. Justice involves holding perpetrators of war crimes, human rights violations, and systemic abuses accountable, both to deter future offenses and to affirm the moral and social norms that sustain peaceful coexistence.

In the Middle East, the challenge of delivering justice is compounded by ongoing conflict, contested governance, and foreign interventions. National judicial systems are often weakened, political pressure can undermine accountability, and social divisions complicate impartial enforcement. Nevertheless, multiple pathways exist: international courts, hybrid tribunals combining local and international expertise, and community-based restorative justice mechanisms. Each of these approaches seeks to prevent cycles of impunity while balancing local legitimacy with broader ethical standards.

Justice also has a preventative dimension. When communities observe that crimes are punished, trust in social and political institutions is reinforced, and the likelihood of retaliatory violence diminishes. Conversely, when justice is absent or selective, grievances fester, resentment spreads, and the risk of renewed conflict escalates. In the Middle East, where grievances have accumulated over generations, justice must be both substantive and credible to contribute meaningfully to peace.

Reconciliation: Rebuilding Social and Moral Bridges

While truth and justice are essential, they alone cannot restore the fractured social fabric. Reconciliation addresses the moral and relational dimensions of conflict, fostering trust, empathy, and cooperation among communities divided by violence or ideology. In the Middle East, reconciliation requires initiatives that engage individuals and communities at the grassroots level: dialogue programs that encourage neighbors to confront past grievances, interfaith initiatives that promote mutual understanding, and restorative justice programs that repair harm and create shared responsibility for coexistence.

Reconciliation is a slow and iterative process. It requires addressing both interpersonal relationships—such as those between families or local communities affected by war—and broader societal relationships, including the trust between citizens and the state. For example, programs that facilitate dialogue between displaced families and host communities can rebuild social bonds eroded by conflict. Similarly, intergenerational initiatives that engage youth in the remembrance of past atrocities, combined with ethical reflection, can instill a sense of shared responsibility and collective commitment to peace.

The moral dimension of reconciliation is particularly important in societies where structural injustice has persisted. By acknowledging past wrongs, fostering accountability, and creating spaces for dialogue, reconciliation restores the ethical foundations necessary for social cohesion. Without this dimension, justice can remain formal and abstract, disconnected from the everyday realities of citizens who continue to live amidst distrust, fear, and trauma.

The Interdependence of Truth, Justice, and Reconciliation

In the Middle East, truth, justice, and reconciliation are deeply interdependent. Without justice, truth-telling can feel hollow, providing acknowledgment without accountability. Without reconciliation, justice may address only legal culpability while failing to rebuild the moral and social relationships that sustain society. When these elements are combined, however, they create a durable foundation for peace that extends beyond elite negotiations and political settlements into the fabric of daily life.

This interdependence also underscores the long-term nature of peacebuilding. TJR is not a one-time intervention or a single program; it is a generational process. Communities must continuously engage in truth-telling, pursue accountability, and invest in reconciliation initiatives to maintain and strengthen social cohesion. In this way, the process becomes a living bridge—a framework through which societies can navigate the complex legacies of conflict, trauma, and displacement.

Applying TJR Principles to the Middle East

Adapting truth, justice, and reconciliation to the Middle East requires sensitivity to ongoing realities. Initiatives must account for:

Ongoing conflict and instability: Programs may need to be localized or phased, starting in areas of relative calm and expanding as security allows.

Cultural and religious contexts: Reconciliation and justice mechanisms should respect local traditions while upholding universal human rights standards.

Displacement and fragmentation: Truth and reconciliation efforts must include refugee populations, displaced communities, and diaspora groups to ensure inclusivity.

Intergenerational engagement: Addressing trauma inherited from previous generations is crucial, incorporating education, storytelling, and youth programs to prevent cycles of violence.

By integrating these considerations, the principles of TJR can provide a roadmap for repairing the moral, social, and political bridges that decades of conflict have fractured. These efforts do not promise immediate peace, but they create the conditions under which sustainable peace can take root.

Truth, justice, and reconciliation are not abstract ideals; they are practical tools for reconstructing the human bridges shattered by conflict. In the Middle East, where war has left communities traumatized, displaced, and divided, implementing these principles is both urgent and complex. Truth validates the experiences of survivors, justice holds perpetrators accountable, and reconciliation restores moral and social bonds. When combined thoughtfully and adapted to local realities, TJR offers a framework for a durable peace that extends beyond ceasefires and treaties into the everyday lives of citizens, rebuilding trust, dignity, and the possibility of coexistence for future generations.

Women as Essential Change-Makers

In conflict-affected societies, women are often the quiet architects of survival and social cohesion. While wars and political negotiations are frequently documented through the lens of diplomacy, military strategy, and elite decision-making, women operate at the grassroots, holding communities together amid chaos. Globally, research and field experience have consistently shown that women's participation in peacebuilding not only strengthens the durability of agreements but also makes them more inclusive and socially sustainable.

In the Middle East, decades of conflict have left millions displaced, entire neighborhoods in ruins, and social structures fragmented. Amid these conditions, women step into multiple roles simultaneously: they serve as educators in refugee camps where children lack formal schooling, coordinate healthcare delivery in regions where hospitals have been destroyed, mediate local disputes between families divided by war, and lead grassroots reconciliation initiatives aimed at repairing social bonds weakened by years of violence.

Their work often addresses the most immediate needs of communities—needs that are invisible in high-level negotiations but vital for sustaining life and rebuilding society. While men may focus on political borders, security arrangements, and the negotiation of ceasefires, women tend to the moral and social scaffolding that allows communities to function. They ensure that children have access to education, that healthcare reaches displaced populations, and that the mechanisms of social trust are maintained even when the broader political system is fractured. In doing so, women create the conditions under which peace can be lived and experienced on a daily basis, beyond the abstract language of treaties and accords.

Supporting women's leadership in both grassroots initiatives and formal peace negotiations is not merely a question of equity—it is a strategic necessity. Evidence shows that peace agreements involving women are more likely to endure and produce tangible social benefits. Women bring perspectives shaped by lived experience, emphasizing reconciliation, dialogue, and inclusivity. They are attuned to the nuances of social relationships and community dynamics, understanding that sustainable peace cannot exist without addressing both material and moral needs.

Women's empowerment also has profound intergenerational effects. In societies where girls witness women taking leadership roles in education, healthcare, mediation, and community organizing, they internalize a sense of agency and responsibility. This fosters a generation capable of engaging constructively in civic life, maintaining social cohesion, and resisting cycles of violence. By modeling leadership, resilience, and moral responsibility, women expand the human capacity for peace beyond immediate interventions and into the long-term fabric of society.

Moreover, women's contributions often extend into spheres of governance and advocacy, bridging gaps between local communities and formal institutions. They lobby for policy changes, advocate for the protection of vulnerable populations, and create networks that connect displaced populations to resources, legal aid, and education.

In doing so, they link the grassroots reality of daily survival with the broader structures of governance, ensuring that the moral and social dimensions of peace are represented alongside political agreements.

In the Middle East, where conflict has fractured trust, displaced millions, and left communities socially and psychologically scarred, women are indispensable change-makers. Their work demonstrates that peace is not only a political condition but also a lived social reality. By nurturing trust, providing essential services, and fostering community resilience, women lay the foundation for durable, inclusive, and morally grounded peace. They do not simply participate in rebuilding society—they are the architects of its restoration, shaping the human bridges that connect communities, generations, and the possibility of a stable future.

Ultimately, recognizing and empowering women as essential actors in peacebuilding is both a moral imperative and a practical necessity. Without their leadership, peace initiatives risk remaining abstract, fragile, or exclusive. With their engagement, societies can rebuild the broken bridges of trust, social cohesion, and intergenerational resilience, ensuring that the foundations of peace endure far beyond the cessation of hostilities.

Youth as Builders of the Future

The youth of the Middle East inherit a landscape scarred by decades of war, displacement, and systemic instability. Across Palestine, Syria, Yemen, and Iraq, adolescents and young adults have grown up amid the constant presence of violence, checkpoints, airstrikes, and the collapse of social infrastructure. Schools lie in ruins, healthcare is intermittent, and the streets they traverse are often sites of insecurity. These young people inherit trauma not only through direct exposure to conflict but also through the intergenerational transmission of fear, loss, and societal fragmentation.

Yet within this context of adversity lies extraordinary resilience and potential. Youth are adaptive; they learn to navigate displacement camps, conflict zones, and fragmented educational systems. They innovate survival strategies, maintain networks of social support, and find ways to continue education and community engagement despite overwhelming challenges. Crucially, they are capable of imagining alternatives to the violent and oppressive systems they inherit. While older generations may be entrenched in cycles of grievance or mistrust, young people often possess the creativity, energy, and openness necessary to envision and construct bridges toward a more peaceful future.

Investing in youth education, vocational skills, and leadership development is therefore central to sustainable peacebuilding. Formal and informal programs that provide access to quality education—even in refugee camps—can counter the sense of hopelessness that pervades conflict-affected communities. Vocational training equips youth with the tools to rebuild their economies and communities, providing tangible pathways toward stability. Leadership programs and dialogue initiatives cultivate negotiation, mediation, and problem-solving skills, preparing young people to participate actively in shaping the societies they will inherit.

Beyond formal programs, youth-led initiatives are especially powerful in bridging social divides. Cultural exchanges, storytelling projects, and inter-community initiatives allow young people from different sects, ethnicities, or regions to share experiences, confront prejudices, and discover common ground. Environmental rebuilding projects, such as reforestation or reconstruction of communal spaces, engage youth in the physical restoration of their communities while fostering a sense of shared responsibility and collaboration. These initiatives create networks of trust and cooperation that adults, entrenched in historical grievances or political constraints, may struggle to establish. In this way, youth act as both beneficiaries and active agents of peace, transforming spaces of trauma into arenas of collaboration and hope.

Inclusion of youth in peacebuilding is not merely symbolic—it is a strategic and moral necessity. Peace processes that exclude young voices risk perpetuating cycles of conflict, leaving grievances unresolved and social fractures unaddressed. Young people who feel alienated or ignored are more likely to be drawn into radicalization, violence, or social apathy, undermining the very foundations of long-term stability. Conversely, when youth are empowered and engaged, they foster communities capable of sustaining dialogue, cooperation, and social cohesion. They become the connective tissue of society, bridging divides, restoring social trust, and embedding resilience into the next generation.

Moreover, youth engagement contributes to intergenerational healing. By providing spaces for expression, leadership, and collaboration, young people are able to process inherited trauma and develop strategies for social restoration. Their participation ensures that peace is not only a political settlement but also a lived, social, and moral reality that resonates across families, neighborhoods, and entire communities. Through mentorship, education, and community projects, youth can transmit values of dialogue, empathy, and constructive engagement to future generations, gradually dismantling cycles of fear, mistrust, and violence.

In the Middle East, youth are both the inheritors of conflict and the architects of its potential resolution. They are uniquely positioned to navigate the complexities of fractured societies, combining resilience with imagination, and experience with the desire for change. By recognizing and supporting their agency, societies can cultivate a generation capable of sustaining peace, rebuilding social cohesion, and ensuring that the bridges fractured by decades of war are reconstructed, strengthened, and maintained for the long term.

Ultimately, the engagement of youth is a cornerstone of durable peace. Their energy, creativity, and moral imagination make them essential participants in the reconstruction of societies torn apart by conflict. Without their inclusion, peace risks being imposed, fragile, and short-lived; with their active participation, it becomes organic, sustainable, and intergenerational, creating a foundation on which the broken bridges of the Middle East can finally be rebuilt.

Bridging the Broken Bridges

Decades of conflict have left the Middle East not only physically scarred but morally and socially fractured. Cities lie in ruins, communities are fragmented, and generations grow up amid trauma, displacement, and uncertainty. The lessons from post-conflict societies such as South Africa, Rwanda, and Northern Ireland offer valuable insights into truth, justice, and reconciliation. Yet the Middle East presents unique challenges that demand tailored solutions—solutions that account for ongoing conflicts, foreign occupations, historical grievances, cultural dynamics, and the staggering scale of human displacement.

Bridging these broken connections requires a holistic approach. Peacebuilding cannot exist in isolation from social, moral, and psychological repair. It must operate alongside political negotiations and humanitarian interventions, integrating them into a framework that addresses both immediate survival and long-term societal cohesion. Humanitarian aid alone can provide food, water, and shelter, but without engagement in truth-telling, accountability, and reconciliation, it cannot repair the deeper fractures that underlie instability. Similarly, political agreements or ceasefires may halt immediate violence, but without moral and social bridges, the risk of renewed conflict persists.

Women and youth are central to this process. They are not passive recipients of aid or beneficiaries of peace agreements; they are essential agents of change. Women, through their leadership in education, health, and community mediation, sustain the everyday rhythms of social life and nurture intergenerational resilience. Youth, with their creativity, energy, and adaptability, bring fresh perspectives and bridge divides between communities fractured by war. Both groups play complementary roles in reconstructing the moral, social, and psychological bridges needed to transform fractured societies into resilient ones.

The process of rebuilding is neither immediate nor linear. Peace in the Middle East is not a singular event—it is incremental, iterative, and often painful. Every story documented, every dialogue facilitated, and every community initiative implemented contributes to the reconstruction of bridges. Grassroots initiatives, such as intergenerational education programs in Palestinian refugee camps, youth-led environmental projects in Syria, or women's mediation committees in Yemen, exemplify this gradual, cumulative approach. These initiatives repair social bonds, foster empathy, and restore dignity at the local level, creating the foundation for broader societal cohesion.

Bridging the broken bridges also requires a cultural and historical lens. Understanding the specific histories of conflict, the patterns of displacement, and the social and religious dynamics of each community is essential. A reconciliation initiative in Baghdad must consider decades of sectarian division, while a youth program in Gaza must navigate the realities of blockade, occupation, and recurrent violence. Solutions must be locally grounded, culturally sensitive, and flexible enough to adapt as circumstances evolve.

The human dimension is critical. Each interaction between communities, each act of listening, and each small gesture of solidarity contributes to reconstructing trust. Trust, dignity, and hope are the metaphoric beams of these bridges—intangible yet essential elements of lasting peace. Rebuilding these bridges requires patience and sustained effort; it is a moral as much as a practical enterprise.

Though these efforts often go unnoticed on the global stage, they carry profound significance for those living in the shadow of conflict. As one Yemeni educator reflects:

"The war broke everything—houses, schools, families. But if we teach our children to listen, to speak, to rebuild, maybe they will inherit bridges instead of rubble. That is our hope. That is our duty."

Her words encapsulate the essence of peacebuilding in the Middle East. Rebuilding is not merely the restoration of infrastructure or the cessation of hostilities—it is the deliberate reconstruction of the human and moral connections that enable society to function, to endure, and to flourish. Each story, each dialogue, and each act of inclusion strengthens these bridges, transforming despair into possibility, fracture into cohesion, and trauma into resilience.

In the end, bridging the broken bridges is a process of collective human effort. It requires collaboration between governments, civil society, communities, and individuals, especially those whose voices have historically been marginalized. The work is ongoing, the path uncertain, but the principle remains clear: peace is built from the ground up, through acts of acknowledgment, justice, dialogue, and empowerment. Only by rebuilding these social, moral, and psychological bridges can the Middle East hope to move beyond the rubble of war toward a future defined by trust, dignity, and hope.

CHAPTER 5

Rebuilding Society

From Ruin to Resilience

The landscapes of the Middle East tell stories of vibrant cities, bustling markets, and thriving communities—stories that now lie partially obscured beneath layers of rubble and dust. Streets that once hummed with the chatter of merchants, the laughter of children, and the rhythm of daily life are scarred by destruction. Aleppo's ancient souks, which had stood for centuries as symbols of culture and commerce, are now fragmented corridors of collapsed walls and shattered windows. In Gaza, neighborhoods once alive with community gatherings and family celebrations have been reduced to skeletal remnants of homes, their residents dispersed into refugee camps or temporary shelters. Sana'a and Mosul, rich with historical heritage and communal life, bear the same testimony: centuries of civilization overshadowed by the immediacy of destruction.

Rebuilding these cities—and the societies that inhabit them—is not merely a technical challenge of reconstruction. The task extends beyond the repair of infrastructure, the laying of roads, or the restoration of electricity and water. It is a moral and social endeavor, requiring attention to the very fabric of community life that war has torn apart. Physical rubble is visible and measurable; social cohesion, trust, and human dignity are far more fragile, yet they are the foundation upon which lasting recovery depends.

Restoring livelihoods is central to this process. War has displaced millions, shuttered businesses, and destroyed local economies. Former artisans in Aleppo's souks may lack the means to return to their trades; farmers along the Tigris and Euphrates in Iraq may find their irrigation systems destroyed or polluted; small business owners in Gaza face restricted movement and limited access to markets. Economic recovery is inseparable from social resilience: without work and income, communities remain trapped in cycles of dependency and despair, unable to invest in the rebuilding of both structures and social ties.

Equally important is the restoration of hope. Decades of conflict have eroded not only infrastructure but the very belief that life can return to normal. Children grow up in displacement camps or neighborhoods surrounded by destruction, absorbing fear, loss, and instability as part of their formative experience. For communities to recover, rebuilding must provide a vision of a future where children can attend schools safely, families can walk streets without fear, and neighbors can collaborate rather than mistrust each other. Hope becomes a resource as essential as food, water, or shelter—it is the glue that holds societies together in the aftermath of violence.

Repairing broken bridges in the Middle East is both literal and metaphorical. Physical bridges, roads, and transportation networks reconnect fragmented communities and restore economic circulation. They allow markets to reopen, aid to reach populations, and displaced families to return to their neighborhoods. But the moral and social bridges are just as crucial. Trust between neighbors, social bonds across sectarian or ethnic lines, and confidence in institutions have been eroded by decades of conflict and injustice. Rebuilding society, therefore, requires deliberate interventions that restore these intangible structures—dialogue programs, community reconciliation initiatives, educational reform, and participatory governance all serve as instruments for reconnecting communities to each other and to the idea of a shared future.

This process is further complicated by ongoing instability. Unlike post-conflict contexts where hostilities have ceased, many parts of the Middle East continue to face sporadic violence, political instability, or foreign interventions. Reconstruction efforts must navigate these uncertainties while remaining forward-looking, ensuring that the work of rebuilding is not undermined by the immediate pressures of insecurity. Projects must be adaptable, culturally sensitive, and inclusive, addressing the needs of the most vulnerable while empowering local populations to lead their own recovery.

Ultimately, rebuilding society in the Middle East is an act of resilience—an assertion that human life, social bonds, and moral cohesion matter as much as walls, roads, or power lines. It is a commitment to restore not only the material trappings of civilization but also the dignity, trust, and hope that war has threatened to erase. Through careful planning, inclusive policies, and the empowerment of local communities—especially women and youth—societies can begin to transform ruins into living spaces of opportunity, reconnecting fractured communities and laying the foundations for a future that is both stable and just.

The challenge is immense, yet the opportunity is profound: to rebuild not just structures, but the social, moral, and psychological bridges that allow societies to heal, endure, and thrive. Every road paved, every school reopened, every market revitalized, and every community dialogue held represents a strand in these bridges—a step toward reconnecting people to one another, to their history, and to the possibility of a shared, resilient future.

Economic Recovery Strategies: Infrastructure, Energy, and Jobs

Economic revival is far more than the restoration of financial systems; it is the lifeblood of sustainable peace. In a region where decades of war have destroyed livelihoods, displaced millions, and disrupted social cohesion, access to work, markets, and basic services forms the bridge between mere survival and the possibility of a dignified, hopeful future. Without these opportunities, communities remain trapped in cycles of dependency, frustration, and vulnerability, unable to translate ceasefires or reconstruction agreements into tangible improvements in daily life.

Post-conflict economies in the Middle East face challenges unlike any in peacetime reconstruction. Roads that once linked towns and markets lie fractured or mined. Electricity grids in Aleppo, Mosul, and Sana'a are unreliable or destroyed. Water networks are contaminated or nonfunctional, and industries—factories, workshops, and small businesses—have been shuttered by years of instability. Markets that once thrived are either abandoned or fragmented. In this environment, economic recovery must balance immediate humanitarian needs with long-term structural development. Relief packages that provide food and temporary work are essential, but they must dovetail with investments in infrastructure, energy, and employment that allow societies to reclaim autonomy and rebuild dignity.

Infrastructure: The Backbone of Recovery

Reconstructing infrastructure is often the most visible and symbolic indicator of societal revival. Roads, bridges, hospitals, schools, and energy grids are not just physical structures; they are conduits for commerce, education, health, and civic engagement. In Mosul, the painstaking restoration of bridges connecting the eastern and western parts of the city has allowed not only the flow of goods but also the reconnection of families and communities long divided by conflict. Similarly, in Aleppo, the rebuilding of school facilities and hospitals is more than an architectural achievement—it is a reclamation of spaces where life, learning, and health can flourish once more.

Infrastructure is also a vehicle for social cohesion. When communities collaborate on rebuilding projects, repairing streets or clearing rubble, they participate in collective acts of agency and solidarity. Each brick laid, each utility restored, and each street reopened becomes a thread in the social fabric, stitching together neighborhoods that war has frayed. Beyond immediate utility, infrastructure serves as a moral and psychological anchor: seeing familiar places restored, children returning to school, and marketplaces reopening signals the possibility of normalcy and the reconstruction of trust.

Energy: Powering Lives and Economies

Energy security is central to economic recovery, but it also holds profound social and symbolic importance. Electricity and fuel power not only factories and water pumps but hospitals, schools, and homes—spaces where human life and community cohesion intersect. In Iraq, the reconstruction of the national electrical grid represents more than kilowatts delivered; it restores the ability of factories to function, schools to operate, and hospitals to provide lifesaving care. In Syria, rehabilitating energy infrastructure in Homs and Aleppo ensures that clinics can refrigerate vaccines, water pumps can operate, and communities can regain a sense of stability in the midst of rebuilding.

Innovative energy solutions can also catalyze employment and local empowerment. In Yemen, decentralized solar microgrids have not only provided electricity to displaced populations but also created new livelihoods for technicians and maintenance crews. This integration of reconstruction with employment demonstrates how energy projects can simultaneously address infrastructure gaps, economic needs, and community agency. Investments in renewable energy—solar, wind, and micro-hydropower—also offer climate-resilient alternatives, ensuring that reconstruction is both durable and sustainable in a region increasingly affected by environmental stressors.

Jobs: The Moral Bridge to Stability

While infrastructure and energy form the backbone of recovery, jobs are the beating heart of community revival. Employment restores dignity, reduces dependency, and allows individuals to participate in the rebuilding of their own lives and neighborhoods. Reconstruction itself—clearing debris, repairing buildings, restoring utilities—can absorb labor on a large scale, offering tangible work for populations long deprived of opportunity.

Beyond immediate reconstruction, broader employment strategies are essential. Microfinance programs, small business grants, and entrepreneurship initiatives allow local markets to reemerge, empower artisans and traders, and stimulate self-sufficiency. Vocational training programs equip youth and women with skills aligned with reconstruction needs: construction, electrical work, plumbing, IT, and healthcare services. Such programs not only provide livelihoods but also foster intergenerational hope, connecting young people to the idea that their futures can be productive, stable, and meaningful.

The connection between economic recovery and social healing cannot be overstated. When communities are employed, educated, and engaged in rebuilding efforts, they are also participating in acts of reconciliation. Trust is rebuilt through shared work, cooperation, and the visible progress of reconstruction. Markets that reopen, roads that reconnect, and utilities that function are more than physical improvements—they are signs that the moral and social bridges torn by conflict can, with effort and care, be restored.

Economic Recovery as Bridge-Building

Ultimately, economic revival in the Middle East is inseparable from the broader task of rebuilding society. Infrastructure, energy, and jobs are not ends in themselves; they are the vehicles through which communities reclaim agency, dignity, and social cohesion. Every paved road, operational hospital, and employed worker represents a thread in the reconstruction of human bridges—bridges that connect families, neighborhoods, and generations to a shared future.

In a region where decades of conflict have fragmented both cities and societies, these economic interventions carry profound moral weight. They are a testament to the possibility of recovery, resilience, and reconciliation. Economic recovery is thus not just a technical task or a financial exercise; it is a moral endeavor, a social intervention, and a practical necessity—all intertwined in the urgent mission to transform rubble into opportunity, despair into hope, and broken societies into resilient communities.

Sustainability and Climate-Smart Reconstruction

Rebuilding the Middle East is not simply about restoring what was lost in war; it is also about preparing communities to survive and thrive amid the pressures of a changing climate. Decades of conflict have already weakened the region's capacity to respond to environmental stressors. Agricultural lands lie fallow or contaminated, water systems are disrupted, and urban centers lack the planning necessary to cope with extreme heat, flooding, or resource scarcity. For populations displaced by war, climate challenges compound vulnerability, turning temporary shelters into precarious environments and increasing the risk of disease, malnutrition, and social tension.

Sustainability in reconstruction is both practical and moral. Infrastructure must not merely replace what was destroyed—it must be resilient to future threats. Roads, homes, schools, hospitals, and utilities rebuilt in the aftermath of war can no longer be constructed as if climate change does not exist. In Iraq, the restoration of irrigation networks in the Mesopotamian plains illustrates this principle. Water, already scarce, is essential not only for food production but for preventing disputes among communities competing for limited resources. Climate-smart irrigation systems—efficient, repairable, and adaptable—serve both as a tool of economic recovery and as a mechanism for maintaining social cohesion, preventing new conflicts from emerging over resources that were once plentiful.

In Syria, climate-conscious reconstruction of housing and public buildings provides families with safety from both the remnants of war and the environmental hazards that threaten them daily. Buildings constructed with heat-resistant materials, improved insulation, and flood-resistant foundations reduce vulnerability to extreme weather events. This is not merely a technical improvement; it is a moral imperative, ensuring that people who have already endured violence are not forced to endure preventable environmental suffering. Families returning to rebuilt neighborhoods gain not only shelter but also dignity and stability, reinforcing the human bridges that reconstruction seeks to restore.

Urban planning and energy infrastructure also play crucial roles in climate-smart reconstruction. Cities like Gaza, Baghdad, and Sana'a require planning that addresses heat islands, stormwater management, and sustainable energy provision. Integration of solar panels, microgrids, and energy-efficient systems reduces reliance on fragile centralized grids while simultaneously creating new job opportunities for local technicians, electricians, and engineers. The reconstruction process thus becomes a nexus of environmental resilience, economic revival, and social stability.

Sustainability extends beyond physical infrastructure to livelihoods and community practices. Agricultural programs in conflict-affected areas that incorporate climate-smart techniques—such as water harvesting, drought-resistant crops, sustainable fisheries, and soil regeneration—equip communities to restore both their economies and their environment. These initiatives have a dual purpose: they enhance food security and income generation while promoting stewardship of the land, encouraging a long-term perspective that war often erodes. Farmers trained in these methods do more than cultivate crops; they cultivate the possibility of lasting peace by stabilizing communities dependent on shared natural resources.

Importantly, climate-smart reconstruction is also about preventing the repetition of past mistakes. Historically, post-conflict reconstruction in the Middle East has often prioritized speed over sustainability. Projects were implemented without accounting for long-term resource scarcity, population growth, or environmental hazards, leaving communities vulnerable once more. By integrating resilience into planning and execution—from green building practices to renewable energy and efficient water management—reconstruction can produce durable, ecologically responsible outcomes that safeguard human life, livelihoods, and dignity.

Rebuilding society in this way is a deeply interconnected task. Infrastructure, livelihoods, and environmental stewardship reinforce one another: water systems support agriculture, agriculture sustains communities, and sustainable urban planning protects public health and social cohesion. Climate-smart reconstruction recognizes that human survival, social trust, and moral recovery are inseparable from the ecosystems that sustain them. In the fractured landscapes of the Middle East, the physical and moral bridges of society cannot endure if they ignore the fragility of the natural environment.

Ultimately, sustainability in post-conflict reconstruction is about resilience at multiple levels. It is about designing communities that can withstand future shocks—whether human-made or environmental—while fostering economic opportunity, social cohesion, and intergenerational hope. In this sense, climate-smart reconstruction is not simply an engineering challenge; it is an ethical and societal imperative, ensuring that the rebuilding of the Middle East does not merely replicate the past but creates a framework for a stable, equitable, and resilient future.

The Role of Education as a Peace Tool

Education is far more than the transmission of knowledge; it is a moral and social instrument capable of reshaping societies fractured by decades of war. In the Middle East, where generations have grown up surrounded by violence, displacement, and insecurity, schools represent fragile islands of normalcy, hope, and potential reconciliation. They are spaces where children and adolescents not only learn arithmetic, language, and science but also absorb the values, norms, and practices necessary to live in a society marked by diversity and division. Education, in this sense, becomes a bridge: it reconnects individuals to their communities, restores trust between generations, and cultivates the foundations of civic life.

Rebuilding educational infrastructure is a critical first step. In Gaza, where schools and universities have been damaged or destroyed during repeated conflicts, youth education programs extend beyond traditional classrooms. These programs integrate psychosocial support, conflict resolution workshops, and community dialogue into daily learning, ensuring that children who have experienced trauma can begin to process their experiences safely. The act of entering a classroom again, of being seen and heard by teachers and peers, offers children a sense of stability and continuity—elements often denied to them by years of conflict.

In Syria, temporary learning centers in displacement camps perform an equally vital role. These centers may be modest, sometimes no more than tents or repurposed community halls, yet they represent hope in the midst of chaos. Children who attend such centers regain a rhythm to their days, an expectation of routine, and an opportunity to reconnect with peers. Education in these contexts functions as a protective measure: it shields young minds from the prolonged psychological impacts of war and prevents a generation from internalizing violence as the norm.

Vocational and technical training is another dimension of education as a peace tool. In Iraq, programs that equip youth with practical skills—such as construction, healthcare, digital literacy, and agriculture—address both economic and social recovery. By providing tangible opportunities for employment, these initiatives reduce the likelihood that frustrated or unemployed youth will be drawn into cycles of radicalization or crime. Moreover, these programs foster collaboration, teamwork, and a sense of purpose, reweaving social bonds that war has frayed. Education in this sense becomes inseparable from economic and moral reconstruction, linking learning to livelihoods and social cohesion simultaneously.

Education also plays a critical role in reconciliation and the rebuilding of moral bridges. Curricula that acknowledge multiple historical and social narratives, encourage critical thinking, and teach conflict resolution can help communities confront past grievances while imagining shared futures. In the Palestinian territories, for example, educational initiatives are beginning to include modules on civic responsibility, empathy, and dialogue, creating spaces where young people can explore their identity in ways that acknowledge suffering while resisting cycles of blame and retaliation. In Yemen and Syria, similar efforts in conflict-affected schools attempt to reconcile fragmented communities by embedding values of tolerance, cooperation, and mutual respect alongside literacy and numeracy.

The long-term significance of education in post-conflict reconstruction cannot be overstated. Schools and training programs serve as incubators for resilience, cultivating a generation capable of sustaining social bridges over time. They nurture the human capital necessary for rebuilding economies, restoring civic life, and participating in governance. More importantly, they instill hope—the sense that life need not be defined solely by loss, displacement, and fear. Each child who returns to school, each youth who gains a skill, and each community that engages in dialogue through education represents a strand in the reconstruction of trust, dignity, and social cohesion.

In the Middle East, where the human bridges of society have been fractured repeatedly by war, education is one of the few interventions capable of simultaneously addressing moral, social, and economic deficits. It restores continuity, cultivates agency, and lays the foundation for a society where peace is more than the absence of violence—it is the presence of opportunity, understanding, and shared responsibility.

Education, therefore, is not merely a tool; it is a bridge, connecting past trauma to future potential, individual recovery to collective healing, and fractured communities to a vision of sustainable peace. In this sense, rebuilding schools, classrooms, and educational programs is as critical to the reconstruction of society as repairing roads, restoring power grids, or reviving local markets—it is a bridge to the future itself.

Technology and Media: Tools for Healing or Division

In the 21st-century Middle East, technology and media occupy a central role in the reconstruction of society. Their impact is dual-edged:

they can either accelerate division or serve as instruments of healing, connection, and reconciliation. Decades of conflict have fractured communities, displaced millions, and disrupted traditional social networks. In such an environment, technology—particularly mobile communications, social media platforms, and digital networks—offers unprecedented opportunities to rebuild human bridges that war has torn apart.

Digital platforms provide access to information, education, and social support for populations scattered across cities, refugee camps, and host countries. In Syria and Iraq, mobile networks allow displaced families to maintain contact with relatives, coordinate access to aid, and participate in telemedicine initiatives that bring healthcare to areas otherwise inaccessible due to insecurity. In Gaza and Yemen, online education programs have become lifelines for children whose schools were destroyed, enabling learning continuity even in the most precarious circumstances. Technology, when responsibly deployed, can restore a sense of agency to communities that have spent years in limbo, bridging physical distances and psychological divides alike.

Media, particularly when localized and community-driven, plays an equally vital role. Documenting the lived experiences of civilians, chronicling survival, and amplifying marginalized voices transforms technology from a neutral tool into a moral instrument of societal reconstruction. In Yemen, youth-led digital storytelling initiatives allow displaced children to narrate their own experiences, offering audiences both within the region and abroad insights into resilience, loss, and hope. These projects do more than share stories—they foster empathy across generations, provide psychological outlets for trauma, and preserve historical memory in ways that official records or foreign reporting often overlook.

Moreover, technology can facilitate dialogue and reconciliation, especially when it connects populations separated by geography, ideology, or sectarian divisions. Online platforms can host moderated discussions between displaced populations and host communities, promote civic engagement, and provide spaces for restorative justice programs to reach participants who may otherwise be isolated. By offering these digital avenues for interaction, technology extends the reach of traditional peacebuilding and community-reconstruction initiatives, creating new forms of social bridges where physical infrastructure has been destroyed.

Yet technology's potential to heal exists alongside its capacity to harm. Unregulated social media and digital platforms can rapidly propagate misinformation, fuel sectarianism, and deepen grievances, particularly in environments already destabilized by conflict. Polarizing narratives, unverified reports of violence, and online harassment can undermine reconciliation efforts, incite violence, or erode trust in institutions and neighbors. In post-conflict societies like Iraq and Lebanon, online platforms have occasionally amplified old divisions, demonstrating that without governance, digital tools can fracture communities further rather than mend them.

Responsible deployment of technology requires deliberate oversight. Media literacy programs are critical to equip communities with the skills to critically assess information and resist manipulation. Civic education, digital ethics, and participatory oversight structures ensure that technology supports peace rather than perpetuating cycles of fear and mistrust. Governments, civil society, and local organizations must collaborate to create regulatory and normative frameworks that balance freedom of expression with the protection of fragile social cohesion.

In the broader context of rebuilding the Middle East, technology and media are not peripheral; they are central to the reconstruction of human and moral bridges. They connect fragmented communities, provide tools for education and livelihood, and preserve narratives of survival and resilience. When paired with ethical governance, inclusive access, and social accountability, these digital tools can accelerate healing, amplify marginalized voices, and foster intergenerational understanding.

Ultimately, the challenge is not technological but social and moral: ensuring that the extraordinary capabilities of digital platforms contribute to the reconstruction of trust, empathy, and social cohesion. In a region where war has repeatedly severed human connections, technology has the potential to act as a bridge—connecting communities to one another, to opportunity, and to the possibility of a shared future. Used wisely, it transforms from a passive medium into an active instrument of peace, reconciliation, and durable societal resilience.

Toward a Reconstructed Society

Rebuilding society in the Middle East is not a single act or a linear process; it is a complex, multidimensional endeavor that intertwines economics, infrastructure, social cohesion, education, and technology. The scars of decades of conflict—rubble-strewn cities, fractured families, and traumatized generations—cannot be repaired by bricks and mortar alone. Reconstruction must reach beyond the physical, addressing the moral, social, and psychological fractures that war has inflicted on communities. Every plan, project, and intervention carries with it the potential to restore not only buildings but human dignity, trust, and hope.

The human bridge—the web of relationships, shared experiences, and communal trust—is central to this reconstruction. In towns across Syria, Iraq, Yemen, and Gaza, communities require safe spaces where they can work together, learn, and reconnect. Markets and workshops, schools and clinics, roads and digital networks are not merely functional assets; they are the scaffolding upon which human interaction and social cohesion are rebuilt. Each repaired street or restored neighborhood represents the physical manifestation of a moral bridge, linking individuals to each other and to the broader society in ways that nurture resilience and belonging.

Women and youth, who have long borne the burden of survival in conflict zones, are not passive recipients of reconstruction; they are its most essential architects. Women lead schools in refugee camps, manage healthcare networks in devastated cities, and organize grassroots reconciliation initiatives that mend fractured communities. Young people, resilient and adaptive despite trauma, contribute by participating in vocational programs, environmental restoration projects, and digital storytelling initiatives that reconnect fragmented societies. Empowering these groups is critical: their agency ensures that reconstruction is not only structural but also social and moral, addressing the very human needs that wars have long ignored.

Economic stability forms the backbone of a reconstructed society. Jobs, vocational training, and restored markets provide more than income—

they restore a sense of purpose and agency. In Baghdad, the restoration of electricity grids has allowed factories to resume production, creating employment opportunities while rebuilding communal confidence. In Yemen, decentralized solar microgrids illuminate displaced populations' homes while training local technicians, linking infrastructure recovery directly to livelihoods and self-sufficiency. Across the region, these projects demonstrate that economic interventions are not isolated acts—they are instruments for reconnecting communities and restoring hope.

Sustainability and climate-smart reconstruction ensure that rebuilding is not temporary or fragile. Water-efficient irrigation in Iraq, flood-resistant housing in Syria, and green urban planning across conflict-affected cities create infrastructure that can withstand both environmental shocks and the pressures of population displacement. Climate-conscious reconstruction links economic revival with ecological stewardship, teaching communities to care for the land even as they rebuild their lives, fostering a deeper sense of shared responsibility and long-term resilience.

Education functions as a bridge between past trauma and future possibility. In Gaza, Syria, and Iraq, schools and training centers provide continuity in learning while fostering critical social skills, conflict-resolution practices, and psychosocial support. They are spaces where young people reclaim the routine, structure, and human connection that war has denied them, cultivating a generation capable of sustaining dialogue, cooperation, and social cohesion over decades.

Technology and media extend the reach of these interventions, connecting displaced populations to educational resources, healthcare, and community networks. Digital platforms allow youth in Yemen to share their stories, Syrian families to participate in dialogue forums, and communities across the Middle East to access telemedicine and e-learning initiatives. Yet these tools must be governed responsibly; without oversight, they risk amplifying division, misinformation, and mistrust. Properly integrated, technology and media become instruments of healing, reinforcing moral and social bridges in fractured societies.

Ultimately, reconstruction in the Middle East is not merely about infrastructure, electricity, or schools; it is about the deliberate, sustained rebuilding of social, moral, and human bridges. When combined with truth-telling, justice, and reconciliation initiatives, these efforts form a foundation for durable peace. Every intervention—restoring electricity in Baghdad, installing a solar microgrid in Yemen, rebuilding classrooms in Aleppo—becomes an act of bridge-building. These are not abstract policies; they are tangible steps toward reconnecting communities to one another, restoring the dignity of populations long marginalized by conflict, and fostering hope that the next generation can inherit bridges rather than rubble.

In this sense, reconstruction is both a practical and moral endeavor. It requires vision, coordination, and courage to address not only the visible ruins of war but also the invisible fractures within human relationships and social structures. The path to a reconstructed society is iterative, incremental, and often painful—but it is also transformative. By integrating economic recovery, sustainability, education, technology, and inclusive social engagement, the Middle East can begin to repair the bridges that conflict has broken, offering a pathway from devastation to resilience, from division to shared possibility, and from despair to enduring hope.

CHAPTER 6

Global Lessons

The Middle East has long been described as a theater of conflict, a region where the fractures of history, ideology, and power converge in ways that ripple far beyond its borders. Decades of wars, occupation, foreign interventions, and internal upheavals have left cities in ruins, societies fragmented, and generations of people living under the shadow of trauma. Yet amid this destruction and human suffering, the region also holds profound lessons for the global community—lessons about resilience, moral responsibility, and the complex architecture of peacebuilding.

These lessons extend beyond geopolitics and strategy. They are deeply human, rooted in the lived experiences of ordinary citizens, displaced families, women and youth, and local leaders who navigate daily realities shaped by violence. They are moral, demanding that the world acknowledge suffering, confront injustice, and recognize the dignity of those often marginalized in international narratives. And they are practical, offering insights into how societies can rebuild, reconcile, and construct bridges—social, economic, and psychological—that connect fractured communities.

The Resilience of Communities

One of the most remarkable features of the Middle East is the resilience of its people. In Syria, despite the destruction of entire neighborhoods and infrastructure, communities have organized informal schooling, healthcare networks, and marketplaces in displacement camps and host cities. In Gaza, local women's cooperatives operate food distribution systems and vocational programs that sustain livelihoods when state services fail. In Yemen, youth-led environmental and energy projects—such as solar microgrids—have not only restored basic services but also cultivated new skills and a sense of agency among displaced populations.

These examples underscore a critical lesson: resilience is a resource as vital as any economic or military asset. Societies may be weakened by conflict, but the ingenuity, solidarity, and determination of communities themselves form the foundation upon which recovery and peace are built. For global actors, this means that interventions must prioritize local leadership and community agency rather than imposing externally determined solutions.

Understanding the Interconnectedness of Conflict

The Middle East also teaches the global community about the interconnectedness of crises. Conflict rarely exists in isolation; economic collapse, displacement, environmental degradation, and political oppression feed into one another. In Iraq, the destruction of water infrastructure has compounded social tensions, while in Yemen, famine and disease exacerbate the human toll of airstrikes and political fragmentation. Failure to address these links often results in partial solutions that cannot break cycles of instability.

Globally, the lesson is that peace and reconstruction require holistic approaches. Economic recovery must be paired with social and educational interventions, environmental resilience, and psychological healing. Political negotiations alone are insufficient; durable peace must also reconstruct the human bridges broken by decades of violence.

Truth, Justice, and Moral Responsibility

A recurring theme across the Middle East is the necessity of truth and justice. Societies where atrocities go unacknowledged—where war crimes, human rights abuses, and corruption remain unaddressed—cannot achieve lasting reconciliation. Historical grievances, if ignored, feed cycles of resentment and retaliation.

The global lesson is both moral and operational: peace is not the mere absence of war. It requires acknowledgment of suffering, accountability for wrongdoing, and structured pathways for reconciliation. Mechanisms such as truth commissions, hybrid courts, and community-based restorative justice programs offer models for addressing grievances in ways that restore human dignity and social trust. Without these moral foundations, bridges rebuilt in physical terms—roads, schools, hospitals—risk remaining disconnected from the human networks they are meant to serve.

Women and Youth as Architects of Peace

Across the region, women and youth emerge as critical agents of reconstruction. They provide continuity where governance has collapsed, lead initiatives that rebuild communities, and foster intergenerational resilience. Women coordinate education, healthcare, and local governance in refugee camps and conflict zones, while young people spearhead vocational, digital, and cultural projects that promote social cohesion and economic recovery.

The global insight is clear: sustainable peace is inclusive. Ignoring the agency and perspectives of women and youth risks reproducing cycles of marginalization and violence. Empowerment of these groups is not optional—it is essential for reconstructing both the social fabric and moral integrity of post-conflict societies.

Technology, Media, and the Responsibility of Information

Technology in the Middle East serves as both a bridge and a barrier. Social media and digital platforms can connect displaced populations, provide access to education and healthcare, and amplify voices often ignored in mainstream narratives. Yet they can also spread misinformation, inflame sectarian tensions, and deepen mistrust.

The global lesson is that technology is not neutral. Its deployment must be paired with media literacy, ethical governance, and community engagement. Digital tools, when responsibly applied, can accelerate reconciliation, document resilience, and restore connections between fractured communities. Mismanaged, they can widen divisions and undermine fragile peacebuilding efforts.

Practical Lessons for the World

From the Middle East, the world learns that:

Resilience is local – Communities themselves are the primary agents of survival and reconstruction. International support must amplify, not replace, local leadership.

Conflict is interconnected – Addressing only political or military dimensions is insufficient; economic, social, environmental, and psychological aspects are equally critical.

Truth and justice are foundational – Durable peace cannot exist without acknowledgment of suffering and mechanisms to hold perpetrators accountable.

Inclusion matters – Women and youth are not passive actors; they are central to social reconstruction and long-term stability.

Technology is a tool, not a solution – Digital platforms can heal or harm; ethical use, literacy, and governance are essential.

Peace is multidimensional – Physical reconstruction, economic recovery, education, environmental resilience, and moral reconciliation must operate in tandem to repair the broken bridges of society.

A Call to Action

The lessons of the Middle East are not abstract. They are a moral and practical guide for policymakers, humanitarian actors, and global citizens alike. Every intervention, whether in education, economic development, infrastructure, or technology, should be seen as an act of bridge-building—repairing the connections severed by violence and creating pathways toward trust, dignity, and shared possibility.

In studying the Middle East, the world is challenged to recognize that rebuilding bridges—literal, social, and moral—is the work of generations. It is painstaking, often incremental, but profoundly necessary. The experiences of communities in Syria, Iraq, Yemen, and Palestine are not only warnings of what happens when bridges collapse; they are also beacons of what is possible when resilience, inclusion, and moral courage guide reconstruction.

The global lesson is clear: understanding and acting on the human, social, and moral dimensions of conflict is not a choice—it is an imperative. In repairing the broken bridges of the Middle East, the world gains insight into repairing the fractures of society everywhere.

Lessons in Human Resilience

Amid the rubble of cities, the dust of displacement camps, and the ongoing echo of airstrikes, the human spirit of the Middle East endures. Resilience in this region is not an abstract concept; it is a daily act of survival, creativity, and communal solidarity that emerges in the most extraordinary circumstances. Families, neighbors, and communities—often with minimal resources—find ways to adapt, rebuild, and maintain a semblance of normalcy even in the shadow of prolonged conflict.

In Palestine, generations of refugees have lived with uncertainty as a constant companion. In sprawling camps such as Baqa'a in Jordan or Shatila in Lebanon, families have transformed temporary shelters into microcosms of society. Children attend makeshift schools, markets thrive on ingenuity and barter, and local health clinics operate with the dedication of volunteers when official systems falter. In these micro-communities, resilience is visible in the simple but profound acts of everyday life: a mother teaching her children literacy while queuing for food, elders mediating disputes to maintain peace within the camp, or youth establishing informal tutoring programs to ensure the continuation of education despite limited infrastructure.

Syria's landscape of resilience is similarly striking. In towns flattened by conflict—Aleppo, Homs, Ghouta—civilians have repurposed rubble-strewn streets as spaces for markets and social gatherings. Neighborhoods without functioning government institutions rely on community committees to distribute aid, protect property, and manage scarce resources. Women often become the linchpins of survival, coordinating food distribution, organizing health services, and sustaining networks of care that keep entire families and communities alive. Youth engage in digital projects that document local history, create educational content, and offer psychological support, showing that even in exile or displacement, the younger generation maintains agency and vision.

Yemen presents a similarly harrowing yet illuminating example. Amid ongoing famine, disease, and destruction, communities have developed localized systems of water management, shared food production, and informal medical care. In regions where state governance has almost entirely collapsed, resilience manifests as decentralized solutions: neighbors teach each other survival skills, women lead vocational cooperatives, and youth implement renewable energy projects to provide electricity for schools and homes. These efforts are not merely survival mechanisms—they are acts of social reconstruction, small bridges connecting communities to each other and to hope.

In Iraq, the story of resilience is tied to both recovery and innovation. After years of conflict that destroyed cities such as Mosul and Ramadi, displaced populations have returned, sometimes rebuilding homes and markets with nothing more than ingenuity and community labor. Informal economic networks flourish, small businesses reopen, and educational initiatives—often organized by local NGOs and civil society actors—equip youth with skills that foster both employment and cohesion.

What these examples collectively demonstrate is that resilience in the Middle East is both moral and practical. It is moral because it sustains dignity, human connection, and community identity in the face of dehumanizing violence. It is practical because it produces tangible outcomes: food on the table, children in classrooms, networks of care, and structures—both literal and social—that allow society to endure.

For the world, the lesson is both urgent and ethical. Humanitarian aid and international interventions cannot succeed if they treat populations as passive recipients of assistance. Instead, effective action must prioritize the agency of local communities, amplify their leadership, and build upon existing mechanisms of resilience. Governments, NGOs, and multilateral organizations have a responsibility to recognize that sustainable reconstruction comes not from imposing solutions from above but from supporting those who have survived and adapted under the harshest conditions.

Education programs, vocational training, and microfinance initiatives are not simply "development tools"; they are instruments of empowerment, restoring autonomy to communities and individuals whose agency has been systematically eroded by war. Investments in local leadership, particularly of women and youth, ensure that reconstruction is inclusive and enduring. When communities are seen as co-creators of their own futures, resilience becomes not just survival, but a foundation for lasting social cohesion, economic revival, and moral reconstruction.

Ultimately, the Middle East teaches the world that human resilience is a bridge over devastation. Even when infrastructure is destroyed, economies collapse, and social trust is fractured, the ingenuity, solidarity, and moral courage of ordinary people offer pathways from ruin to reconstruction. In recognizing and supporting this resilience, global actors do not merely deliver aid—they participate in the rebuilding of broken bridges, enabling societies to restore trust, dignity, and hope for generations to come.

The Interconnectedness of Conflict

The Middle East offers a stark and sobering lesson: conflict is rarely a single, isolated phenomenon. Wars, political oppression, economic collapse, and environmental degradation do not exist in silos—they interact, reinforce one another, and create cascading cycles of instability. Understanding these dynamics is essential for anyone seeking to grasp not only the region's challenges but also the broader lessons it holds for the world.

Consider Yemen, a country where multiple crises converge. Airstrikes have destroyed schools, hospitals, and marketplaces, leaving communities without access to basic services. The ongoing blockade and conflict have disrupted supply chains, driving food prices up and creating widespread famine. At the same time, climate stress—rising temperatures, water scarcity, and desertification—exacerbates these vulnerabilities, compounding the difficulty of survival for displaced populations. In this context, a single intervention, such as sending food aid or rebuilding a school, cannot address the full scope of human suffering. Each crisis feeds into the next: malnutrition weakens communities' ability to work or attend school, destroyed infrastructure limits access to healthcare, and environmental degradation increases competition over scarce resources, sometimes triggering further conflict.

In Syria, the interplay of political violence, displacement, and economic collapse illustrates a similar pattern. When neighborhoods are bombed or blockaded, families flee, swelling refugee camps in neighboring countries and creating new pressures on infrastructure and social systems. Markets shrink, unemployment rises, and informal economies struggle to sustain families. Environmental damage—from the destruction of water systems, agricultural land, and sanitation networks—further compounds the crisis. The result is a self-reinforcing cycle: insecurity drives poverty, poverty fuels social tension, and social tension sustains instability.

Iraq provides another lens. Years of sectarian conflict, foreign occupation, and insurgency have left cities in ruin and communities fragmented. Destruction of electricity grids and water systems diminishes industrial output and public services, weakening trust in governance. Unemployment and economic stagnation, in turn, create fertile ground for radicalization and renewed violence. Environmental degradation, including polluted rivers and desertification, further threatens food security and human health. Here, too, the crises are intertwined, each amplifying the others.

What these examples reveal is a broader truth: the Middle East illustrates the systemic nature of conflict. Violence cannot be disentangled from displacement, economic collapse, environmental stress, or social fragmentation. Each dimension interacts with the others, creating feedback loops that make recovery extraordinarily complex.

For the global community, this interconnectedness carries an urgent lesson. Peace and stability cannot be achieved through piecemeal interventions. Building schools without ensuring security may leave children exposed to violence. Providing humanitarian aid without restoring economic systems may create dependency without resilience. Negotiating ceasefires without addressing social, environmental, and historical grievances may yield temporary calm but not durable peace. Interventions must adopt a holistic perspective—what practitioners often call "systems thinking"—that identifies root causes, anticipates ripple effects, and addresses multiple dimensions of conflict simultaneously.

Understanding the Middle East thus teaches that broken bridges cannot be mended one plank at a time. Physical reconstruction, social cohesion, economic recovery, and moral repair must be pursued together, each reinforcing the other. By attending to the interconnectedness of conflict, policymakers, humanitarian actors, and communities themselves can design strategies that do not merely treat the symptoms of war but reconstruct the foundations of society, restoring trust, dignity, and opportunity.

Ultimately, the region's experience challenges the world to think differently about conflict. Peace is not merely the absence of bombs or political agreements; it is a multidimensional process that requires addressing the economic, environmental, social, and moral fractures that wars leave behind. The Middle East, in all its complexity, offers a living case study of how crises are interwoven and how the reconstruction of broken bridges demands integrated, thoughtful, and compassionate strategies.

The Importance of Truth, Justice, and Reconciliation

In the Middle East, the scars of war are not only physical—they are moral, psychological, and intergenerational. Cities lie in ruins, but even more profound are the fractures in social trust, collective memory, and the sense of justice that binds communities together. These fractures are rarely accidental; they are often the cumulative result of unacknowledged atrocities, unpunished crimes, and a historical record that marginalizes victims. Understanding the moral dimension of conflict is essential, because rebuilding bridges—both social and psychological—requires confronting these deep-rooted injustices.

Syria exemplifies the devastating consequences of unaddressed wrongdoing. Bombings of civilian neighborhoods, chemical attacks, and deliberate targeting of hospitals have left millions of survivors traumatized. For decades, perpetrators of violence often acted without accountability, while victims navigated the collapse of institutions designed to protect them. The absence of truth-telling mechanisms means that grievances fester, mistrust becomes intergenerational, and reconciliation remains fragile. Communities cannot rebuild if the human stories of loss and survival are erased or ignored.

In Iraq, decades of occupation, sectarian conflict, and insurgency created layers of unresolved injustice. Families who lost homes, livelihoods, or loved ones often found no recourse. Trials were sporadic, accountability partial, and historical narratives contested or suppressed. The moral gap—the space between suffering and acknowledgment—became as destructive as any bombed-out street or shattered school.

Palestine presents yet another lens. Generations of displacement, occupation, and episodic violence have created a complex matrix of grievances. Without acknowledgment of historical injustices, including dispossession, restrictions on movement, and systematic marginalization, cycles of anger, resistance, and retaliation continue. Victims experience not only the immediate violence but the compounding weight of invisibility: their experiences are often excluded from global narratives or reduced to abstract statistics.

The lesson for the world is profound: peace is more than the cessation of hostilities. True and lasting peace requires **truth**, **justice**, and **reconciliation** as foundational pillars. Truth demands that survivors and witnesses have the ability to recount experiences without fear or obstruction, ensuring that human suffering is recognized and memorialized. Justice requires mechanisms—whether domestic courts, international tribunals, or hybrid models—that hold perpetrators accountable, affirming the principle that violence has consequences and that impunity erodes the moral foundations of society. Reconciliation involves structured efforts to repair social bonds, facilitate dialogue between divided communities, and restore trust that has been eroded by conflict and oppression.

Implementing these principles in the Middle East is extraordinarily challenging. Conflicts are ongoing, institutions are weak, and power imbalances are entrenched. Yet even partial efforts—community truth commissions, local restorative justice programs, interfaith dialogues— can create vital pathways toward rebuilding. Recognition of suffering, even if limited, signals that victims are seen and heard, offering a moral anchor around which fractured communities can begin to coalesce.

The experience of the Middle East underscores that **bridges cannot be rebuilt without confronting the fractures beneath them**. Physical reconstruction, economic development, and humanitarian aid are essential, but without moral repair—acknowledgment, accountability, and reconciliation—these efforts risk remaining superficial. Societies may appear to recover in infrastructure, but the human connections that sustain community and collective identity remain vulnerable.

For global observers and policymakers, the lesson is clear: interventions must address not only the material consequences of conflict but also its moral dimensions. Supporting truth-telling initiatives, facilitating accountability for human rights violations, and promoting reconciliation programs are not abstract ideals—they are essential strategies for breaking cycles of violence, restoring human dignity, and reconstructing the bridges that connect past trauma to future possibility.

In the end, the Middle East teaches that **peace without justice is incomplete, and justice without reconciliation is fragile**. Only by integrating these principles can societies hope to repair the moral, social, and psychological bridges that have been broken by decades of conflict, creating the foundations for durable, inclusive, and human-centered peace.

Inclusivity: Women and Youth as Change-Makers

The Middle East's path to recovery is not paved solely by political agreements or economic investments—it is shaped by the people who inhabit its streets, camps, and neighborhoods. Among the most vital agents of change are women and youth, whose contributions to social cohesion, education, and community resilience are often underrecognized yet indispensable. Their work exemplifies the principle that rebuilding broken bridges requires inclusivity at every level.

Women in conflict-affected areas often carry responsibilities that extend far beyond traditional roles. In Gaza, they manage schools and community learning centers, ensuring that children receive both education and psychosocial support despite frequent disruptions from violence and blockade. In Syria, women coordinate local healthcare services, provide maternal and child care in displacement camps, and organize neighborhood networks to distribute aid and maintain public hygiene. Even amid rubble and insecurity, women maintain continuity in family life and community functioning, creating networks of trust and stability where formal governance has collapsed. Their presence transforms recovery efforts from simple survival into social reconstruction, fostering a moral and relational foundation that allows communities to endure.

Youth, too, play an essential role as architects of the future. In Iraq, young people develop vocational programs and technical workshops to equip peers with marketable skills that support both livelihoods and social cohesion. In Yemen, displaced adolescents lead environmental restoration projects, replanting degraded land, constructing small-scale solar grids, and introducing innovative solutions to water scarcity. Digital storytelling initiatives, particularly in Syria and Palestine, allow youth to document local histories, share personal experiences of conflict, and foster intergenerational dialogue. These efforts not only preserve memory but also create bridges of understanding across fractured communities.

The collective impact of women and youth extends beyond individual programs; it transforms the social fabric itself. Their involvement ensures that reconstruction is not top-down but participatory, responsive to local needs, and morally grounded. Schools, healthcare networks, vocational centers, and community initiatives become nodes in a broader social network, reinforcing bonds of trust, dignity, and cooperation that have been eroded by years of conflict.

For global actors—governments, NGOs, and multilateral organizations—this lesson is critical. Development and peacebuilding efforts that fail to include women, youth, and local leaders are not merely incomplete; they risk perpetuating cycles of marginalization and conflict. Excluding these groups undermines the moral and social bridges that sustain community resilience and leaves initiatives vulnerable to failure. Inclusivity, therefore, is not optional; it is foundational to sustainable peace.

The Middle East demonstrates that empowerment and participation are essential to breaking cycles of trauma. When women and youth are given authority, responsibility, and resources, they become agents of healing and innovation. They restore not only the infrastructure of daily life but also the intangible connections—trust, hope, and moral legitimacy—that form the true foundation of society. These lessons carry a universal significance: any society seeking to recover from conflict must recognize that lasting peace is inseparable from inclusivity. Without it, bridges remain broken; with it, societies gain the capacity to transform trauma into opportunity and despair into collective resilience.

In essence, the experiences of women and youth in the Middle East remind the world that reconstruction is as much about human capital as it is about physical capital. The repair of broken bridges—between individuals, communities, and generations—requires acknowledging, empowering, and amplifying the voices of those who have historically borne the heaviest burdens of conflict. Their participation ensures that peace is not only achievable but enduring, anchored in the lived realities, creativity, and moral courage of the very people who must inhabit the societies being rebuilt.

Lessons in Technology and Media

The Middle East offers a profound illustration of technology's dual nature: it can heal or it can harm, bridge communities or deepen divisions. In a region where conflict has fractured societies, uprooted millions, and destabilized governments, digital platforms have emerged as both lifelines and battlegrounds for ideas, narratives, and influence. Understanding this duality is essential for global actors, policymakers, and communities seeking to navigate reconstruction and reconciliation.

On the one hand, technology has provided critical tools for survival, education, and community rebuilding. In Syria, displaced children in temporary learning centers access online classrooms and educational materials that would otherwise be unavailable. Telemedicine platforms in Yemen and Iraq enable healthcare workers to reach remote or conflict-affected populations, providing treatment, counseling, and training that transcend geographic and security barriers. Social media and digital storytelling projects allow Palestinians, Syrians, and Iraqis to preserve oral histories, document local experiences, and transmit lessons of resilience to broader audiences. These technological applications create virtual bridges where physical infrastructure may be destroyed, allowing communities to maintain social cohesion and a sense of shared identity despite displacement and violence.

At the same time, the Middle East illustrates the risks inherent in unregulated or ethically ambiguous use of technology. Digital platforms can amplify sectarian narratives, spread misinformation, and inflame tensions in environments already vulnerable to polarization. During periods of political unrest or armed conflict, false information about attacks, political movements, or displaced populations can trigger mass panic, retaliatory violence, or further mistrust between communities. In Palestine and Iraq, online content has at times been weaponized to reinforce grievances or manipulate perceptions, illustrating how media can become a tool of division rather than reconciliation.

For global actors and local stakeholders alike, the lesson is clear: technology is not inherently neutral. Its impact is determined by governance, ethical design, and the social context in which it operates. Digital platforms must be paired with media literacy initiatives, education programs, and community engagement strategies that encourage critical thinking, empathy, and constructive dialogue. Policies that ensure transparency, accountability, and local ownership of narratives are essential to prevent the reinforcement of pre-existing fractures.

The Middle East also demonstrates that technology can serve as a catalyst for intergenerational healing. Youth-led digital initiatives— storytelling, environmental monitoring, or educational content creation—provide young people with agency in reconstructing their communities. By documenting their experiences, they not only process trauma but also educate peers and foster cross-community understanding. Similarly, women-led online networks provide access to training, entrepreneurship opportunities, and advocacy channels that strengthen social resilience and inclusion.

Ultimately, the region teaches a broader lesson: digital tools are extensions of human intention, and their ethical deployment is a prerequisite for sustainable peace. Technology can amplify the voices of the marginalized, preserve collective memory, and enable dialogue across divides, but without conscious, values-driven intervention, it can also perpetuate cycles of mistrust and conflict.

For the world, the Middle East offers a cautionary yet hopeful model: technology, when paired with literacy, governance, and community-centered approaches, can reconstruct moral and social bridges as effectively as it restores physical connections. In the context of broken bridges—rubble-strewn streets, displaced populations, and fractured societies—digital platforms, ethical media, and informed engagement become essential instruments for repairing connections, restoring dignity, and fostering long-term resilience.

Reader's Action Guide: Practical Steps

The Middle East, with its layers of historical, political, and social complexity, offers lessons that extend far beyond regional borders. Its stories of destruction, resilience, and hope challenge every reader to reflect not only on distant conflicts but also on their own capacity for action. The broken bridges of cities, communities, and moral authority in the Middle East are mirrored in fractured societies worldwide. Recognizing this, individual engagement—however modest—becomes part of the global effort to foster peace and justice.

Educate Yourself and Others

Understanding the Middle East requires moving beyond headlines and soundbites. Deep engagement with credible sources on history, culture, conflict dynamics, and human stories builds empathy and informed judgment. Education is the first bridge a reader can build: connecting knowledge to compassion. Sharing insights within families, schools, and professional networks multiplies impact, fostering communities that are informed, attentive, and morally conscious.

Support Local Initiatives

Communities on the frontlines of conflict are not passive recipients of aid—they are agents of their own survival and reconstruction. By supporting local initiatives—schools, health clinics, vocational programs, or peacebuilding organizations—readers can amplify grassroots change. Prioritizing programs led by women and youth ensures that contributions strengthen the social foundations necessary for long-term stability. Micro-grants, volunteer efforts, or advocacy for funding local NGOs all serve as practical forms of bridge-building.

Advocate for Holistic Policy

Conflicts in the Middle East reveal that isolated interventions rarely succeed. Violence, displacement, economic collapse, environmental degradation, and political oppression are intertwined. Readers can engage by advocating for policies that address these interconnected challenges. This includes lobbying for comprehensive foreign aid that integrates humanitarian relief with education, infrastructure, and environmental resilience, as well as supporting diplomatic approaches that consider social and moral dimensions of peace, not just territorial or strategic outcomes.

Engage in Digital Responsibility

Technology and media, as shown across the region, can be instruments of either division or healing. Responsible digital engagement involves promoting media literacy, critically assessing sources, and ensuring that online platforms amplify truth rather than misinformation. Supporting digital initiatives that foster dialogue, preserve historical memory, and give voice to marginalized communities can transform virtual spaces into sites of reconciliation rather than conflict.

Invest in Education

Education serves as both a practical tool and a moral bridge. By contributing to programs that provide access to schooling, vocational training, and psychosocial support, readers help reconstruct the social and intellectual foundations necessary for long-term peace. Educational investments nurture the next generation of leaders, thinkers, and innovators who can sustain societal resilience and prevent the inheritance of trauma.

Promote Dialogue and Empathy

Bridge-building begins with understanding. Readers can participate in or support intercultural dialogues, workshops, or community initiatives that connect people across social, religious, or ethnic divides. Even small-scale engagement—listening, learning, and facilitating communication—reflects the same principles necessary for repairing fractured societies in conflict zones. Empathy and dialogue are the human glue that binds communities together, preventing cycles of violence from repeating.

A Final Reflection: Rebuilding Bridges in a Fractured World

The Middle East, scarred by decades of war, occupation, and political turbulence, stands as both a warning and a lesson for the world. Its cities bear the physical wounds of conflict—Aleppo's streets shattered, Gaza's neighborhoods leveled, Sana'a's ancient quarters fractured, and Mosul's historic districts reduced to rubble. But beyond the visible devastation lies a deeper truth: the moral, social, and psychological bridges that connect people to each other, to opportunity, and to hope are often the most fragile. The region reminds us that the cost of conflict is not only measured in destroyed buildings or displaced populations but in fractured trust, broken social bonds, and the long shadow of generational trauma.

Yet even amidst the devastation, the Middle East offers a story of resilience and human ingenuity. Communities, often with minimal resources, continue to reconstruct their lives. Women in refugee camps operate makeshift schools and health clinics, providing stability and continuity where formal institutions have collapsed. Youth take initiative in rebuilding local infrastructure, launching digital storytelling projects, or restoring degraded lands. Neighbors engage in dialogue, cross-sectarian cooperation, and small acts of everyday reconciliation that challenge cycles of mistrust and revenge. These efforts are not simply reactions to necessity—they are acts of moral courage, social reconstruction, and bridge-building.

The lessons from the Middle East extend far beyond its borders. They teach that peace is not merely the absence of violence; it is the deliberate cultivation of justice, dignity, opportunity, and collective responsibility. True peace requires acknowledging past wrongs, creating mechanisms for accountability, restoring disrupted social bonds, and empowering communities to participate actively in rebuilding their societies. It is as much a moral endeavor as a political one, demanding attention to both the structures of governance and the intangible networks of trust and empathy that bind people together.

CHAPTER 7

Unbroken Bridge

Vision for a Peaceful Middle East

The Middle East is a land of profound contradictions. It is at once a cradle of civilization and a theater of repeated destruction; a region rich in culture, history, and human ingenuity, yet one where cities bear the physical scars of decades of war and communities are fractured by ideology, sectarianism, and geopolitical rivalries. Streets in Aleppo, Gaza, Mosul, and Sana'a tell the stories of lives interrupted, homes lost, and futures deferred. The landscapes themselves are monuments to conflict, yet within them lies the potential for renewal, for the construction of bridges that are moral, social, and physical in nature.

A vision for a peaceful Middle East is not an abstract ideal; it is a framework rooted in pragmatism, morality, and human agency. The unbroken bridge is more than symbolism—it is a conceptual and operational approach to rebuilding society, reconnecting communities, and fostering resilience across generations. This bridge rests on both visible and invisible foundations: roads, schools, hospitals, and energy grids on the one hand; trust, dialogue, empathy, and shared purpose on the other.

Beyond Military Intervention

History demonstrates that military victories alone cannot produce lasting peace. Top-down diplomacy, imposed ceasefires, or externally brokered agreements often fail to address the deeper fractures embedded within communities. True peace requires a multidimensional strategy that confronts the root causes of conflict, engages the daily realities of civilians, and reconstructs both the moral and social scaffolding of society. Economic recovery, education, justice, and environmental sustainability are not optional—they are essential pillars in the bridge toward durable peace.

Lessons from the World

Globally, post-conflict societies provide lessons without offering exact templates. South Africa's Truth and Reconciliation Commission illustrated how public acknowledgment of suffering can restore dignity and rebuild social trust after decades of oppression. Rwanda's community gacaca courts highlighted the power of local participation in justice mechanisms, showing that accountability and reconciliation can coexist. Northern Ireland's experience underscored the delicate balance between political compromise and community-level reconciliation, demonstrating that peace must be negotiated both in government halls and in neighborhoods where distrust runs deep.

For the Middle East, these models are instructive but must be adapted. Unlike these contexts, the region faces ongoing conflicts, foreign occupations, environmental pressures, and complex sectarian divides. Peacebuilding cannot be a one-size-fits-all formula; it must respect cultural norms, understand historical grievances, and amplify the agency of those whose lives have been most affected by war.

Women and Youth as Foundational Agents

At the heart of this vision are women and young people. In refugee camps across Syria, Palestine, and Yemen, women operate schools, coordinate health services, and organize community reconciliation initiatives, sustaining daily life when formal institutions fail. Their labor is often invisible, yet it forms the backbone of social stability, nurturing resilience in families and communities.

Youth, similarly, embody both the inheritance of trauma and the potential for transformation. In Iraq and Yemen, young people engage in environmental restoration, digital storytelling, vocational training, and civic programs. These initiatives do more than occupy time— they restore agency, rebuild livelihoods, and reconnect fractured communities. Excluding the perspectives of women and youth risks perpetuating cycles of trauma, mistrust, and inequality; including them is essential to creating an intergenerational bridge to peace.

Economic Recovery and Infrastructure

Economic stability is a central pillar of the unbroken bridge. Decades of war have destroyed infrastructure, disrupted markets, and decimated livelihoods. Roads, bridges, electricity networks, hospitals, and schools are not merely physical structures; they are the conduits of opportunity, dignity, and social cohesion. In Iraq, restoring the electrical grid enables factories to operate and schools to function; in Syria, rehabilitating water and sanitation systems reduces disease and fosters trust in communal governance. Job creation, vocational training, and microenterprise support are equally critical, providing immediate livelihoods while embedding social purpose into reconstruction.

Sustainability and Climate Resilience

Reconstruction in the Middle East cannot ignore the realities of climate change. Water scarcity, desertification, and extreme heat compound vulnerability, particularly for displaced populations. Climate-smart reconstruction—green building practices, solar energy, sustainable agriculture, and resilient urban planning—ensures that rebuilt societies are prepared for future shocks. In Iraq, restoring irrigation networks in the Mesopotamian plains prevents intercommunal disputes over scarce resources. In Syria, rebuilding homes with climate-resilient materials protects families from floods and heatwaves. Integrating environmental resilience into recovery planning strengthens both social stability and economic viability.

Education as a Moral and Social Bridge

Education serves as both a practical and moral foundation for peace. Schools are spaces where children learn not only literacy and numeracy but also the principles of empathy, dialogue, and shared responsibility. In Gaza, psychosocial support and conflict resolution training are integrated into youth programs, giving children tools to process trauma and engage constructively with their communities. In Syria, temporary learning centers in displacement camps provide stability amid chaos. In Iraq, vocational and technical training equips young people with skills for reconstruction, reducing the risk of frustration translating into radicalization. Education is the bridge that carries future generations across the chasm of inherited trauma.

Technology and Media as Instruments of Reconciliation

In the 21st-century Middle East, technology and media have dual potential. Digital platforms can amplify stories of resilience, provide educational resources, and facilitate dialogue among displaced populations and host communities. Yet the same tools can spread misinformation, reinforce sectarianism, and exacerbate polarization. Responsible use of technology—paired with media literacy, ethical oversight, and community engagement—can transform it into a bridge rather than a wedge, connecting communities across fractured spaces and preserving collective memory.

Truth, Justice, and Reconciliation

At the core of the unbroken bridge lies moral accountability. Truth-telling, justice, and reconciliation are indispensable to breaking cycles of violence. Communities must confront past atrocities, recognize shared suffering, and build mechanisms of accountability ranging from local initiatives to international courts. Without addressing these moral fractures, peace remains fragile, and the specter of renewed conflict persists. A durable peace requires that justice and reconciliation be intertwined, forming the foundation upon which all other reconstruction efforts rest.

The Unbroken Bridge as Collective Endeavor

Ultimately, the unbroken bridge is a living construct—a continuous project of engagement, moral responsibility, and social reconstruction. It encompasses roads, schools, energy systems, and water networks, but it also embodies dialogue, empathy, trust, and opportunity. Every repaired infrastructure, restored service, and reconciled community represents a plank in a bridge connecting past trauma to a future of dignity, stability, and hope. Women and youth, economic revival, climate resilience, education, and technology all converge to form this comprehensive vision.

The Middle East teaches the world a profound lesson: rebuilding broken bridges is never linear or immediate, but through deliberate, inclusive, and holistic action, societies can transform devastation into resilience. Peace is not a single moment or event—it is the enduring labor of repairing moral, social, and physical connections, ensuring that future generations inherit not rubble, but bridges to shared opportunity and a sustainable future.

Final Reflection – Building the Bridge Together

The Middle East stands as both a testament to human suffering and a monument to resilience. Decades of war have left physical and moral landscapes fractured: cities reduced to rubble, neighborhoods emptied by displacement, and communities scarred by trauma passed down through generations. Yet amid this devastation, the region offers an enduring lesson: peace is not a singular event, a signed treaty, or a fleeting ceasefire. Peace is a process—gradual, continuous, and deeply collaborative—requiring patience, courage, and persistent human effort.

Every act of reconstruction, whether tangible or intangible, contributes to the repair of the fractured bridges connecting people, communities, and nations. Rebuilding a school in Aleppo does more than restore a physical structure; it revives the rhythm of childhood, restores a sense of normalcy, and reconnects children to a collective future. Establishing solar microgrids in Yemen brings electricity to displaced populations, but it also revitalizes local economies, strengthens social cohesion, and nurtures dignity where despair once prevailed. Facilitating interfaith dialogues in Baghdad may seem small against the backdrop of decades-long sectarian violence, yet these conversations reconstruct the moral and social scaffolding essential for coexistence. Each initiative, regardless of scale, becomes a plank in the larger bridge of societal repair.

Bridge-building is inherently both collective and individual. Policymakers, humanitarian workers, educators, activists, and global citizens each hold a stake in the process. A single act—training youth in vocational skills, mentoring women to lead community programs, or supporting local entrepreneurial ventures—ripples outward, connecting fractured networks, empowering marginalized voices, and reinforcing social resilience. In the Middle East, these micro-level efforts intersect with macro-level interventions, such as international aid programs, governance reforms, and peace negotiations, creating a layered and comprehensive architecture for sustainable peace.

Central to this endeavor are **women and youth**, whose roles transcend survival. Women are the keepers of social cohesion, running schools, clinics, and community reconciliation programs, sustaining life when formal structures fail. Youth embody both the inheritance of conflict and the potential for transformation, engaging in environmental restoration, digital storytelling, vocational training, and civic initiatives that rebuild the social fabric. Their participation is not supplementary; it is foundational. When women and youth are empowered as architects of peace, societies are far more likely to cultivate durable, equitable, and resilient futures.

The unbroken bridge extends beyond infrastructure and governance; it encompasses **human dignity, moral accountability, and social cohesion**. Communities must be empowered to define their own futures, to share and validate their experiences of suffering, and to participate actively in reconstructing their societies. Truth-telling, justice, and reconciliation are indispensable elements of this moral architecture. A repaired road, a rebuilt school, or restored neighborhood is a step forward—but without addressing historical grievances, human rights violations, and cycles of intergenerational trauma, physical reconstruction alone cannot achieve lasting peace.

The Middle East demonstrates that bridges—physical, social, or moral—do not repair themselves automatically. They demand deliberate attention, sustained labor, and collective responsibility. Broken bridges, whether destroyed by bombs or eroded by mistrust, can be rebuilt, but only through commitment, empathy, and justice. Recognizing the human consequences of conflict is essential; understanding shared suffering becomes the foundation upon which cooperation and reconciliation are constructed.

The vision of an **unbroken bridge** is simultaneously pragmatic and aspirational. It acknowledges the scars of the past while charting a path toward a future in which communities are connected, dignity is restored, and generations inherit not rubble but opportunity. It calls upon every individual—whether living in the Middle East or observing from afar—to engage in bridge-building: to sustain dialogue, invest in education, support inclusive initiatives, and amplify voices that have historically been marginalized. Each action, no matter how small, becomes a plank in a living bridge, reinforcing the structure of social, moral, and communal repair.

History teaches that the labor of peace is continuous. Bridges are never complete; they require ongoing maintenance, vigilance, and adaptation to evolving challenges. Yet this very incompleteness offers hope: every repaired road, rebuilt school, reconciled community, and empowered individual demonstrates that restoration is attainable, that societies can rise from destruction, and that the human capacity to forgive, rebuild, and hope is enduring.

Ultimately, the **Middle East embodies a universal lesson**: broken bridges—whether between neighbors, communities, or nations—can be mended through deliberate, sustained, and inclusive effort. The act of rebuilding is both a moral imperative and a practical necessity. Each initiative, whether localized or systemic, contributes to a structure that is resilient, adaptive, and unbroken—a bridge that connects the past to the future, trauma to healing, and despair to hope.

Peace, therefore, is not a destination. It is the cumulative labor of countless individuals, communities, and institutions working together, spanning divides and connecting fragments of society. The unbroken bridge is a testament to humanity's capacity to reconstruct what has been destroyed, to restore what has been lost, and to believe in the possibility of a Middle East—and a world—where dignity, justice, and shared futures prevail.

This book closes with an invitation: the rebuilding of bridges—physical, social, and moral—is the responsibility of every individual, institution, and nation. Policymakers, educators, humanitarian actors, and citizens alike can contribute: by investing in education, supporting women and youth, fostering dialogue, promoting ethical technology, and advocating for justice. These steps ripple outward, reinforcing local initiatives and shaping a broader culture of peace.

The bridge is never complete. Its planks require constant attention. But every repaired road, rebuilt school, reconciled community, and empowered individual strengthens its structure. The Middle East teaches the world that hope is a practice, resilience is a habit, and peace is a labor of commitment, courage, and compassion.

And in that labor lies humanity's greatest promise: that even in regions scarred by conflict, societies can rebuild, communities can reconnect, and generations can inherit opportunity instead of devastation. The unbroken bridge is possible. It is attainable. And it begins with the deliberate, sustained, and collective work of people determined to believe in—and build—a better future.

For the global reader, the region becomes a mirror reflecting our own responsibilities. Understanding the Middle East requires more than passive observation; it calls for ethical engagement, informed action, and sustained reflection. Every step matters: educating oneself about history and culture, supporting locally driven initiatives, advocating for policies that address interconnected economic, social, and environmental challenges, using technology responsibly to foster connection rather than division, investing in education, and promoting dialogue and empathy. Each of these actions, no matter how small, contributes to repairing broken bridges—bridges that span not only the Middle East but also fractured communities and societies worldwide.

Importantly, these bridges—whether physical, social, or moral—are never permanent. They demand continuous care, intentional effort, and resilience against both natural and human-made challenges. Neglect or indifference can allow the fractures of the past to reemerge, while sustained attention can transform the legacies of conflict into opportunities for growth, cohesion, and shared human flourishing.

Ultimately, the Middle East teaches a profound and urgent truth: the human capacity for rebuilding, healing, and connection endures even in the shadow of devastation. By embracing the lessons of resilience, inclusivity, accountability, and ethical engagement, societies everywhere can begin to repair their own broken bridges. The work is never complete, yet it is always necessary—an ongoing moral, social, and practical endeavor that reaffirms the possibility of peace, hope, and a shared future for all.

Closing Section: The Bridge Awaits

For too long, the story of the Middle East has been told in the language of collapse. We speak of the wars that shattered nations, the treaties that faltered, the alliances that cracked under strain. We remember bridges that once stood proudly only to fall into rivers of mistrust and rubble. At times, it seems the region's history is written not in ink but in dust — the dust of fallen walls, scattered families, broken promises.

And yet, a bridge is never entirely gone, even when destroyed. Its outlines remain in memory and stone. The foundations sink deep into the earth, reminders of what was once possible. Every broken span whispers the same question: will we leave this crossing in ruins, or will we try again?

This book has walked us across many wreckages: colonial legacies that divided lands, conflicts that displaced millions, environmental destruction that scarred both earth and soul. We have listened to voices from Syria, Yemen, Palestine, Israel, Iraq, and Iran — voices of mothers, teachers, children, and doctors — and we have seen how war is measured not only in casualties but in generations of trauma. We have examined the paradox of America, at times a builder, at times a breaker, and always an actor whose presence is felt across the region's riverbanks.

But we cannot end with collapse. To speak only of ruins is to deny the possibility of repair. If history is the story of broken bridges, then the future must be the story of rebuilding. The question is not whether bridges can be rebuilt — they can. The question is who will carry the stones, who will lift the beams, and whether they will be laid carefully enough to endure.

The answer lies with three groups who hold the power of construction: the leaders who must draft and fund the design, the youth who must provide the muscle and imagination to raise it, and the next generation who will walk upon it. And, beyond them, the entire human community, for no crossing of such magnitude can stand on one nation's effort alone.

The time has come to shift our gaze from rubble to foundation, from despair to repair. The bridge awaits. But it does not await passively — it calls.

Bridges rise or fall on the courage of those who lead. Leaders are more than diplomats at tables or generals at war rooms; they are the architects of possibility. Their choices determine whether families return home, whether children drink clean water, whether hope is planted in place of rubble.

History offers rare but shining moments when leaders chose courage over convenience. In 1977, Egyptian President Anwar Sadat boarded a plane to Jerusalem. His journey was a shock not only to his own people but to the world. No Arab leader had ever stood in Israel's parliament, let alone spoken of peace. "I come to you with an open heart," he said, his words carrying the weight of decades of war. That step across the void was bold, untested, and dangerous. But it worked. Together with Israeli Prime Minister Menachem Begin and guided by U.S. President Jimmy Carter, Sadat's leap produced the Camp David Accords. It ended three decades of enmity between Egypt and Israel.

That bridge, narrow and fragile in its infancy, has endured more than four decades. It has weathered wars, uprisings, and political storms, yet it stands — a testament to what is possible when leaders take risks not for power but for peace. Sadat paid with his life, assassinated for his audacity. Yet his crossing changed the map of the Middle East forever.

Years later, in 1993, Israeli Prime Minister Yitzhak Rabin and Palestinian leader Yasser Arafat shook hands on the White House lawn. Between them stood U.S. President Bill Clinton, his arms outstretched, his smile broad. The handshake was awkward, stiff, but its symbolism was electric. It represented a bridge long imagined but never crossed — the bridge between two peoples locked in cycles of displacement and violence. The Oslo Accords that followed faltered under the weight of assassinations, suicide bombings, and expanding settlements. Yet for a moment, the image of Rabin and Arafat showed that even the deepest divides could be faced with vision.

King Hussein of Jordan, too, made his choice. In 1994, he signed a peace treaty with Israel, ending decades of hostility. He spoke not in the language of conquest but of responsibility: a responsibility to his people and to generations yet unborn. His decision was pragmatic, but also moral. Jordan, a small kingdom surrounded by storms, chose to anchor itself to peace. His crossing remains intact today.

These examples remind us that leadership is not measured by the ease of choices but by their cost. It is easy to maintain hostility, to preserve the status quo of fear. It takes greater courage to step into uncharted territory, to risk political survival for the sake of future stability. Leaders are remembered not for the wars they fought but for the bridges they dared to build.

Yet leadership is not only about bold gestures or high ceremonies. A bridge is more than its opening day; it requires maintenance, inspection, reinforcement. Leaders who wish to be remembered as builders must invest in the practical, often unglamorous work of repair. That means rebuilding schools in Aleppo, restoring olive groves in Palestine, decontaminating rivers in Iraq, replanting orchards in Yemen. It means ensuring that treaties are not just signatures on paper but lived realities in villages and cities.

Leaders must also recognize that bridges are not built for photo opportunities; they are built for people. Signing a peace agreement is meaningless if displaced families remain in camps, if jobless youth turn to despair, if polluted land poisons the next harvest. True leadership asks not only: "Can I secure peace on paper?" but also: "Will a mother find medicine for her child tomorrow? Will a child walk to school in safety?"

And leadership requires listening. No bridge will stand if built from above alone. Leaders must invite civil society, women's groups, religious voices, and young activists to the table. Bridges built only by elites collapse when ordinary people feel excluded. Bridges built with community input endure, for they carry not just policy but legitimacy.

The architects of tomorrow's crossing must therefore think not in terms of power but of permanence. The question is not, "How do I win today?" but "What will endure for my children tomorrow?" Sadat, Rabin, Hussein — they left lessons carved in stone. The leaders of today and tomorrow hold the tools. They can draft designs that repair not only borders but also lives, not only treaties but also trust.

They are the architects of the bridge that waits.

The Bridge Awaits

History shows us again and again that bridges are never accidents. They do not appear in the mist like miracles. They are drawn by vision, anchored by courage, and lifted into place by many hands. Across the Middle East, bridges have collapsed so often that some have grown skeptical that they can be rebuilt at all. Colonial ambitions broke them; wars and occupations blasted them apart; fear and suspicion eroded their foundations. Yet even in ruins, the outline remains. The idea of connection—the possibility of crossing—still lingers. And if there is one truth that unites all these fractured stories, it is this: the broken bridge is not the end.

Leaders stand at the banks of history with choices heavier than stone. Their decisions are not abstract: they determine whether families return home, whether rivers are cleaned, whether schools rise from rubble. When leaders act with vision, bridges emerge.

Consider Anwar Sadat's journey to Jerusalem in 1977. Against the advice of many and amid enormous personal risk, he stood before the Israeli Knesset and spoke words that reshaped history. His courage, matched by Menachem Begin's willingness to respond, produced the Camp David Accords—the first lasting peace between Israel and an Arab state. That bridge, though narrow and fragile at first, still carries two nations across decades of tension.

Or recall Yitzhak Rabin and Yasser Arafat on the White House lawn in 1993, guided by Bill Clinton's outstretched hands. That handshake— awkward, strained, but unforgettable—became an emblem of possibility. The Oslo process faltered in later years, its scaffolding shaken by violence and mistrust, but in that moment, a bridge was visible to the entire world.

Leaders also have the power to repair what violence has shattered. King Hussein of Jordan, who signed peace with Israel in 1994, spoke often of his people's suffering and his determination that future generations should inherit something better. His legacy reminds us that leadership is not only about defending borders but about expanding horizons.

Today's leaders hold the same tools. Their responsibility is heavier, for they face not only the ruins of past conflicts but also the added burdens of displacement, economic stagnation, environmental collapse, and generational trauma. Their task is to design bridges that last—not just in treaties and ceremonies but in the lived realities of their citizens. That means investing in housing for refugees, ensuring that young people have meaningful work, restoring water systems and farmland, and creating justice mechanisms that address wounds without reopening them. Leadership is not only about securing victory. It is about securing peace that can endure.

The Power of Youth

If leaders draft the blueprints, youth raise the beams. Their energy, creativity, and impatience with old barriers make them natural builders. Across the region, young people are already creating bridges, often in the most unlikely places.

In **Gaza**, amid blockade and hardship, youth-led NGOs have emerged to teach coding, languages, and entrepreneurship. Young people who once saw only walls now design apps and launch startups that connect them to the wider world. In their innovation is a refusal to let isolation define them.

In **Iraq**, after years of conflict, young entrepreneurs in Baghdad and Basra are turning abandoned warehouses into tech hubs and cultural centers. They are transforming ruins into spaces of imagination, proving that creativity can reclaim even the most scarred landscapes.

Programs like **Seeds of Peace** bring together Israeli and Arab teenagers in neutral spaces where they live, talk, and argue together. These encounters do not erase differences, but they build friendships and memories strong enough to challenge stereotypes. Years later, many of these participants become journalists, teachers, lawyers, or politicians—and they carry with them a vision of the other side that is human, not faceless.

In **Iran**, young environmental activists organize clean-up campaigns along polluted rivers and lakes, linking ecological repair to civic renewal. They understand that healing the land is part of healing society. And in **Lebanon**, youth collectives have led relief efforts in times of crisis, distributing food and medicine when institutions falter.

Each of these actions may seem small. A mural painted on a damaged wall, a coding class taught in a darkened room, a youth dialogue circle in a rented hall—these are not treaties or armies. But they are planks of the bridge. They are proof that even in the midst of conflict, connection is possible.

Beyond the youth stands the next generation—the children who watch, who listen, who ask. Their questions reveal the stakes with heartbreaking clarity.

In Aleppo, a little girl once asked her mother why the sky was dangerous. In Gaza, a boy wondered why the water in his glass ran brown. In Tel Aviv, a girl clutched her father's hand in a bomb shelter and whispered, "When can I go outside again?" These are not political statements. They are the unvarnished truths of childhood lived under shadow.

These children are the ultimate test of our work. They will inherit the bridges we build—or the ruins we abandon. If leaders and youth repair crossings with vision, the next generation will know futures defined not by war but by commerce, culture, and community. They will grow up learning languages instead of slogans, cultivating orchards instead of clearing rubble, building companies instead of militias. If we fail, they will inherit cycles of fear and trauma, condemned to repeat the lessons we refused to learn.

The broken bridge is, in this sense, a moral ledger. What we build or neglect today determines whether the next generation lives on ruins or on roads that lead somewhere new.

The work of rebuilding cannot be done by one side alone. No bridge will hold if one hand builds while another tears down. Its strength must come from many directions—Arab and Israeli, Iranian and Iraqi, Yemeni and Syrian, Palestinian and Lebanese, American, European, Asian, and African.

The bridge of the Middle East is not merely a local structure. Its collapse has shaped the world through refugee crises, energy shocks, terrorism, and global insecurity. Its reconstruction will also reverberate outward, bringing stability not only to the region but to the entire international order.

This is why blame must be laid down. Blame is heavy stone, and stone left unplaced becomes rubble. Responsibility, on the other hand, is the mortar of bridges. To point fingers is to remain on opposite banks. To join hands is to begin crossing together.

And so we return to the image that has guided this book: the broken bridge. It stretches across the chasm of history, its beams fractured, its planks fallen, its stones scattered. Yet its foundations endure. The bridge has not vanished. It waits.

It waits for leaders to summon courage. It waits for youth to offer imagination. It waits for the next generation to inherit something stronger than ruins. And it waits for all of us, beyond the region, to see that we too are part of the work. To read is to witness. To witness is to decide.

Will we leave the bridge unfinished, another monument to failure? Or will we build, patiently and together, until it is strong enough to carry us all—past and future, fear and hope, war and peace—across to the other side?

The bridge awaits. The choice is ours.